Get Up and Move with Nonfiction

Get Up and Move with Nonfiction

Grades 4-8

Nancy Polette

An imprint of Libraries Unlimited
Westport, Connecticut • London

Library of Congress Cataloging-in-Publication Data

Polette, Nancy.
  Get up and move with nonfiction / Nancy Polette.
     p. cm.
  Includes bibliographical references and index.
  ISBN 978-1-59158-661-6 (alk. paper)
  1. Reading promotion—United States. 2. Children's literature—Study and teaching—Activity programs—United States. 3. Books and reading—United States. I. Title.
  Z1003.2.P65   2008
  028.5'5—dc22   2007041517

British Library Cataloguing in Publication Data is available.

Copyright © 2008 by Nancy Polette

All rights reserved. No part of this book may be reproduced
in any form or by any electronic or mechanical means, including
information storage and retrieval systems, without permission in
writing from the publisher, except by a reviewer, who may quote brief
passages in a review. Reproducible pages may be copied for classroom
and educational programs only.

Library of Congress Catalog Card Number: 2007041517
ISBN-13: 978-1-59158-661-6

First published in 2008

Libraries Unlimited/Teacher Ideas Press, 88 Post Road West, Westport, CT 06881
A Member of the Greenwood Publishing Group, Inc.
www.lu.com

Printed in the United States of America

The paper used in this book complies with the
Permanent Paper Standard issued by the National
Information Standards Organization (Z39.48–1984).

10 9 8 7 6 5 4 3 2 1

Contents

Introduction ix

Part One: Science
   Knowledge Circle 3
   My Name Is 5
   Here Is My 6
   Busy Scientist 7
   Department Store 8
   Two Handed Animal Expert 9
   Simile Guess 10
   Living Food Chain 11
   The Conducted Research Report 12
   Alliteration Race 13
   Two Headed Expert 14
   Planets Circle Story 15
   Planets: Information 17
   Good Reading: Astronomy 18
   Animal Circle Story 19
   Moving Like an Animal 20
   Good Reading: Animals 21
   Dinosaur Circle Story 22
   What Was It? Prehistoric Creatures 23
   Good Reading: Prehistoric Creatures 24
   Be an Inventor 25
   Good Advice 26
   Title Stories: Science 27
   Science Titles 28
   More Science Titles 29
   The Added Phrase Science Report 30
   What Color Is It? 32
   Readers Theatre: Luther Burbank 33
   Readers Theatre: Maria Mitchell 35
   Readers Theatre: Jonas Salk 37
   Readers Theatre Outline 39

Part Two: Mathematics

　　Warm Up Games 45
　　What's Your Excuse? 46
　　It's All In a Word 47
　　Geometry Match 48
　　Definitions for Geometry Match 49
　　Math Quotes 50
　　More Math Quotations 51
　　Mathematician Mix-Up 52
　　Title Stories: Math 53
　　Math Titles 54
　　More Math Titles 55
　　Sequels to Math Tales 56
　　More Sequels to Math Tales 57
　　The I Have, Who Has Game: Archimedes 58
　　The I Have, Who Has Game: Ada Lovelace 59
　　The I Have, Who Has Game: Robert Goddard 60
　　The I Have, Who Has Game: Bill Gates 61
　　A Math Play to Figure Out and Perform 62
　　A Math Play to Figure Out 64
　　Good Reading: Mathematics 67

Part Three: Geography

　　Explorers 71
　　A Gift For the Queen 72
　　Geography Terms 73
　　Categories 74
　　Places in the World 75
　　Alphabet Travels 76
　　Introductions 77
　　My Aunt Came Back 78
　　Circle Games 79
　　Meet a Landform 80
　　Meet a Weather Phenomenon 81
　　The Tic Tac Geography Excuse 82
　　A Preposition Prairie 83
　　Singing About Rivers 84
　　Rivers, Oceans, and Seas 85
　　A Rhyming Arctic Adventure 86
　　Create an Environment 87
　　The Fifty States 88

Mnemonics Challenge 89
The Mystery Game. 90
Comparing Countries 91
Giant Sentences 92
Canadian Where Am I? 93
Tourist Attraction. 94
Storytelling in Geography 95
Strange Destinations 97
Destinations. 98
What Color Is It? 100
Speaking German. 101
Speaking Strine 102
Play World Traveler. 104
World Bingo 105
Good Reading: Places in the World. 106

Part Four: U.S. History
U.S. History Book Reviews 109
History Told Two Words at a Time 115
Who Said That? 116
More Quotations 117
The Poetry Line Story 118
Title Stories: American History 119
History Titles 120
More History Titles 121
Sequels to History 122
Stop the Action. 125
The Start and the Finish 126
The Shortest Possible Story 127
The Shortest Possible Nonfiction Account. 128
The ABCs of History 129
Change of Mood. 132
Point of View 133
Mixed Up History 135
Only One! 139
Whose Tale Is True?: Davy Crockett 140
Whose Tale Is True?: William F. Cody 142
Whose Tale Is True?: Annie Oakley. 144
Whose Tale Is True?: Clara Barton 146
Whose Tale Is True?: Calamity Jane 148

Transforming Narrative Into Dialogue! 150
Frontier Towns. 151
Nonfiction Booktalks to Mark and Perform 153
Good Reading: American History 155

Index 159

Introduction

Reading, research, and writing begin with INTEREST! Here are more than 140 fun pre-reading and writing activities to stimulate interest in a variety of subject areas. Players explore biography as they compete to name famous people within specific categories. Matching halves of nonfiction titles that don't match can lead to creative skits; a variety of titles in science, math, and history are introduced using mime; circle stories are presented that require both research and originality; math plays need to be completed before they are performed; creating sequels to history has never been so much fun!

Get Up and Move with Nonfiction is a unique approach to motivating students to reading, writing, and research. Players become actively involved with the topic as curiousity and interest build in specific subject areas. Many students who may not be the best readers are often the best at readers' theatre and improvisation, since they are given the freedom to perform within flexible guidelines. In addition, students will:

- Meet and solve real life problems

- Use associative thinking throughout the subject areas

- Solve math problems and apply solutions to readers' theatre

- Increase vocabulary in science, math, geography, and history

- Create circle stories with factual material

- Develop creative tales using titles from science and social studies

- Tell nonfiction accounts two words at a time

- Use quotations from historical figures in unusual ways

- Create original excuses using vocabulary from science and geography

- Use factual material in songs, chants, giant sentences, and mystery games

- Create sequels to history

- Transform narrative into dialogue

- Combine events from historical eras into original scenarios

- Assume the role of eyewitness to historical events

- And much more!

Part One

Science

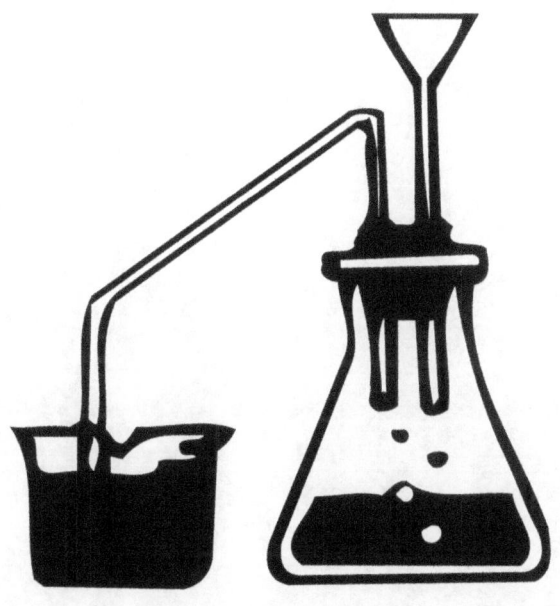

Eureka! At last there is a cure for . . .

KNOWLEDGE CIRCLE

Setting: Classroom or gym

Number of Players: Entire group.

Objective: To allow students to speak from any knowledge they have about topics named by the leader. Topics can include people, places, or animals.

Procedure: Form two circles, one within the other. When music plays the outer circle walks counter clockwise and the inner circle walks clockwise. When the music stops, the leader calls out the topic. Players talk with each other, telling what they know about the topic. When the music starts, the talk ceases and the circles move again repeating the sequence until four to six topics have been discussed.

Suggested Topics:

ANIMALS	ASTRONOMY	GEOLOGY
Badger	Andromeda	Desert
Bear	Altair	Dinosaur
Beaver	Aquarius	Earth
Bighorn	Aries	Earthquake
Bobcat	Betelgeuse	Erosion
Buffalo	Big Dipper	Flood
Caribou	Black Holes	Fossil
Chipmunk	Cosmos	Geography
Copperhead	Earth	Glacier
Coyote	Jupiter	Ice Age
Deer	Little Dipper	Lava
Gila Monster	Mars	Mineral
Gopher	Mercury	Mountain
Grizzly Bear	Mira	Plains
Jack Rabbit	Moon	Prehistoric Animal
Moose	Neptune	Prehistoric Man
Mountain Lion	North Star	Rock
Muskrat	Observatory	Volcano
Opossum	Pluto	
Porcupine	Saturn	
Prairie Dog	Sun	
Raccoon	Universe	
Rattlesnake	Uranus	
Skunk	Venus	
Squirrel		
Wolf		
Woodchuck		

May be copied for classroom use. *From Get Up and Move with Nonfiction* by Nancy Polette. Westport, CT: Teacher Ideas Press. Copyright © 2008.

The X Game

Choose a word. Make lines for each letter.
Classmates guess the letters until the word is revealed.

___ ___ ___ ___ ___ ___

Good Reading: *Hidden Worlds: Looking Through a Scientist's Microscope* by Stephen Kramer. Houghton-Mifflin, 2001.

MY NAME IS . . .

Objective: To understand that science has many different branches and to be able to define the various areas of scientific study.

Procedure: Each player takes the part of a scientist from one of the fields listed below. One player begins by introducing himself or herself and gives his or her area of study as one of the scientists. The player then states two things that the scientist would learn about in his or her work. The two items should begin with the first letter of the scientist's field. Players can be as creative as they wish in their introductions.

Follow Up: Introduce books within various science areas.

Astronomy	Chemistry	Physics
Bacteriology	Geology	Space Science
Biology	Medical Science	Zoology
Botany	Meteorology	

Examples:

Listen up, all you people! My name is [player's name] and I am sometimes called a rock hound, but I study **geology** learning about **glaciers** and **geophysics**.

Hello! Hello! My name is [player's name] and I like chasing things like bacteria that cannot be seen by the human eye. I study **bacteriology** and learn about **bacteria** and tiny **bugs** you can't see.

Hi there! My name is [player's name] and I like growing plants. I study **botany** and learn all about **buttercups** and **bitterroot**.

Come see all my fancy machines. My name is [player's name] and I can tell you all about **meteorology**. I predict the weather including **monsoons** and **monstrous ice storms**.

Good Reading: *Scientist Ask Questions* by Ginger Garrett. Children's Press, 2004.

HERE IS MY . . .

Number of Players: Eight

Objective: To become familiar with areas of science and to effectively pantomime an object associated with a particular area.

Procedure: Each player chooses the role of a scientist and an object associated with that person. In turn, each player stands before the group and using a large trash bag, creates the object. No words are spoken. The audience must guess the object and the person who uses it. The character must then pantomime the object so that the group can guess what the area of study is and what the object is.

Follow Up: Introduce books in various science areas.

DOCTOR	THERMOMETER
BIOLOGIST	MICROSCOPE
ASTRONOMER	TELESCOPE
PHYSICIST	INCLINED PLANE
ZOOLOGIST	COMPUTER SIMULATIONS
BOTANIST	FLOWER
CHEMIST	TEST TUBE
GEOLOGIST	ROCK HAMMER

Choose one of the objects above. Tell or show how many other things the object could be used for, other than its intended purpose.

Good Reading: *How to Think Like a Scientist* by Stephen Kramer. HarperCollins, 1997.

BUSY SCIENTIST

Number of Players: Five

Objective: To define those tools used in various scientific pursuits.

Directions: Teams must research the tools used by the scientist in one of the fields below. The leader calls out the name of one of these scientists.

Follow Up: Introduce biographies of famous scientists in several fields.

GEOLOGIST   BOTANIST   BIOLOGIST   ZOOLOGIST

(Any other scientific field can be used)

Player One (without speaking) comes on stage and demonstrates one object the scientist might be working with. The audience must guess the object.

Player Two enters and mimes the first object and (without speaking) demonstrates a second object the scientist would use. The audience must guess the second object.

Player Three enters and mimes the first two objects and (without speaking) demonstrates a third object the scientist would use. The audience must guess the third object.

Player Four enters and mimes the first three objects and (without speaking) demonstrates a fourth object the scientist would use. The audience must guess the fourth object.

Player Five enters and mimes the first four objects and (without speaking) demonstrates a fifth object the scientist would use. The audience must guess the fifth object.

Helpful Hints:
The first time the game is played a team can be given the scientist's laboratory in advance and team members can discuss which object will be mimed.

A large plastic trash bag can be used to demonstrate the objects, if desired. Team members who are self conscious in demonstrating the objects will concentrate on what to do with the trash bag rather than themselves.

Good Reading: *Science Discoveries on the Net* by Anthony Fredericks. Libraries Unlimited, 2000

DEPARTMENT STORE

Number of Players: Six

Objective: To associate the tools of a scientist with his or her field of study.

Directions: One player takes the part of the person in charge of the department store information desk. This person has a list (but not a description) of scientific items for sale in the department store.

In turn, each scientist approaches the desk and describes the object he or she is looking for in the store. The name of the object cannot be given.

The information clerk and the scientist carry on a dialogue in which the clerk tries to get the scientist to give a more complete description of the object. When the clerk guesses the object correctly, he/she directs the scientist to the area in the store where the object can be purchased.

Before playing the game the player must research a complete description of the item to be described including various uses.

Follow Up: Introduce biographies of famous scientists in several fields.

Examples: (Tools of any scientist can be used)

CHEMIST
    Test tube: glass vial for holding liquids
    Bunsen burner: gas burner for heating elements
    Microscope: series of reflective mirrors to increase image size
    Spectrometer: separates substances according to the mass of their ions

BOTANIST
    Trowel: for digging earth around plants
    Paraffin Wax: to embed plants for study
    Microtome: slices thin sections of plants
    Phytotron: controls the environment of plants

GEOLOGIST
    Igneous rocks: crystalline or glassy rocks formed when magma cools
    Sedimentary rocks: found near Earth's surface, products of weathering
    Metamorphic rocks: altered by temperature or pressure, change in mineral content
    Contour Maps: show the elevation of the Earth's layers
    Spectrometer: determines the ages of rocks

Good Reading: *Science Is . . .* by Susan Bosak. Firefly Books, 2000.

TWO HANDED ANIMAL EXPERT

Number of Players: Teams of three.

Objective: To recall and orally report information on several related animals.

Procedure: One player takes the part of the interviewer. A second player takes the part of the animal expert. The animal expert answers questions asked by the interviewer about his or her area of expertise. Another player kneels behind the expert and acts out appropriate hand gestures.

Follow Up: Introduce books about animal look-alikes.

ALIKE AND DIFFERENT	
Rabbits	Hares
Frogs	Toads
Butterflies	Moths
Crocodiles	Alligators
Rats	Mice
Dolphins	Porpoises

Good Reading: *Alligators and Crocodiles* by Karen Dudley. Raintree, 1997; *Where Did the Butterfly Get Its Name? Questions and Answers About Butterflies and Moths* by Melvin Berger. Scholastic, 2005.

SIMILE GUESS

Number of Players: Two

Objective: To describe the characteristics of animals that are often mistaken for each other using similes.

Procedure: Player one describes one characteristic of an animal using a simile. Player two describes one characteristic of an animal using a simile. In turn the players continue the descriptions, one characteristic at a time. After any description the audience can guess which animal is being described.

Animal pairs to use: rabbit / hare; frog / toad; moth / butterfly; crocodile / alligator; rat / mouse; dolphin / porpoise

Example: frog / toad

Player #1 Its eyes bulge out like_____ (frog)

Player #2 Its body is as stubby as_____ (toad)

Player #1 Its webbed hind feet are as long as_____ (frog)

Player #2 Its skin is as dry as_____ (toad)

Player #1 Its skin is as slimy as_____ (frog)

Player #2 Poison glands behind the eyes look like_____ (toad)

Player #1 Its eggs are clustered like_____ (frog)

Player #2 Its eggs are in long chains like_____ (toad)

Good Reading: *Crinkleroot's Guide to Knowing Animal Habitats* by Jim Arnosky. Simon & Schuster, 1997.

LIVING FOOD CHAIN

Number of Players: Will vary depending on the food chain.

Objective: To understand the concept of food chains.

Procedure: Players will take the parts of plants and animals in a food chain and act out their parts without dialogue. The audience must identify the players and the food chain.

Possible Scenarios:

Grasshopper eats the dandelion
Caterpillar eats the grasshopper
Frog eats the caterpillar
Snake eats the frog
Owl eats the snake

Bees pollinate the clover
Cow eats the clover
People drink milk

Frog eats the grasshopper
Snake eats the frog
Hawk eats the snake

Mouse eats the wheat
Snake eats the mouse
Owl eats the snake

ADD MORE FOOD CHAINS

Good Reading: *Who Eats What? Food Chains and Food Webs* by Patricia Lauber. HarperCollins, 1995.

THE CONDUCTED RESEARCH REPORT

Number of Players: Six

Objective: To understand and explain a scientific topic.

Procedure: Five players will research a topic in science. One player will act as the conductor. At a signal from the conductor, player one begins discussing the topic. The conductor moves, in any order, from one player to another. Players must continue speaking as if there were no pause. Players who are not speaking must listen carefully. Each must have the next word ready to go. The scenario continues until the conductor indicates the end. A time limit of two to three minutes is suggested.

Possible Topics:

Atoms and Molecules	Rain Forest
Photosynthesis	Hurricanes, Typhoons, and Cyclones
Carnivores and Herbivores	The Respiratory System
Physics of Why and How Things Move	Solids, Liquids, and Gasses
Earthquakes and Volcanoes	The Milky Way and Other Galaxies
A Food Web	Tsunamis
Plants With and Without Seeds	Nature of Sound and How We Hear
How Animals Move	Types and Formation of Rocks
The Planets in Our Solar System	Origins and Principles of Light
How Electricity Works	The Water Cycle

ALLITERATION RACE

Number of Players: Two teams of six players each.

Objective: To explain a scientific topic using alliteration.

Procedure: Students submit words related to a science topic currently under study. Words are placed in a basket or box. A leader selects a word and directs the word to Team One. Team members, speaking one at a time, must, in one minute, say a five or six word alliterative sentence about the topic. If Team One is successful the team receives five points. Then a different word is selected and given to Team Two. The game continues until each team has received five words. The team with the most points wins.

Example:

ASTRONOMY WORDS		
Altair	Aquarius	Asteroid
Betelgeuse	Big Dipper	Black Holes
Constellation	Cosmos	Earth
Galaxy	Jupiter	Little Dipper
Mars	Mercury	Mira
Moon	Neptune	North Star
Observatory	Pluto	Saturn
Sun	Universe	Venus

TWO HEADED EXPERT

Number of Players: Three

Objective: To report information on a science topic.

Procedure: One player interviews an expert on a chosen subject in science. The expert is played by two other players. The experts reply to the interviewer's questions (which can be prepared in advance) taking turns and giving one sentence at a time.

Example: The Human Body

Interviewer: What are the basic needs of the human body?

Expert One: Humans can survive a few weeks without food and a few days without water.

Expert Two: But humans can survive only a few minutes without air.

Interviewer: Tell me about body weight.

Expert One: Muscles make up about half the human body weight.

Expert Two: Weight is gained if more calories are taken in than used in daily activity.

Expert One: People's skin weighs twice as much as their brains.

Expert Two: Sugars and fats add more to body weight than vegetables.

Interviewer: What can you tell us about the human heart?

Expert One: The healthy human heart beats more than 36 million times a year.

Expert Two: Cholesterol can clog arteries and prevent the flow of blood to the heart.

Variation

"Experts" might describe the water cycle, the food chain, photosynthesis, or almost any other science topic.

Good Reading: *See For Yourself: More than 100 Experiments for Science Fairs and Projects* by Vicki Cobb. Scholastic, 2001.

PLANETS CIRCLE STORY

Objective: Students will show understanding of a nonfiction topic by encoding the information in a new form.

Procedure: Four students will use information found on page 17 and any additional information they may find in creating a circle story about four planets The story must include description, location, and two or three additional facts—including one negative fact. Be sure to tell why the planet would want to become a different planet.

Follow Up: Introduce books on astronomy.

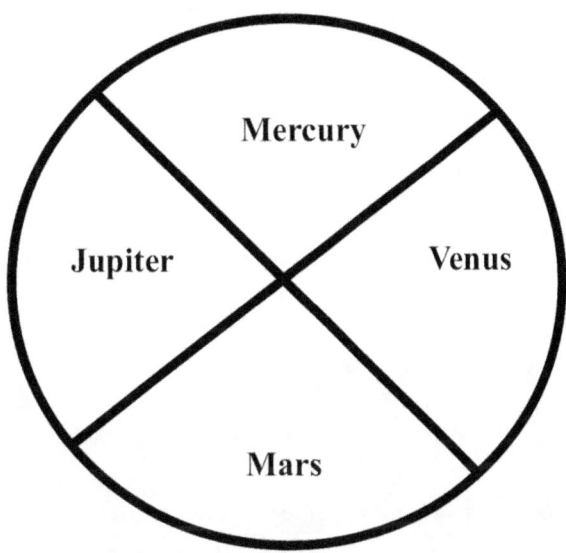

Example:

My name is **Mercury** and since I am closest to the sun I am one hot, stretched-out planet. To cool off I race around the sun as fast as I can. The trip takes 88 days compared to the poky Earth that takes 365 days to do the same thing. I've run out of sunscreen and the sun is really hot. I'll ask the Planet Master to let me become **Venus.**

I am **Venus,** the second planet from the sun. Would you believe that a single day (the time it takes me to turn around once) is 243 Earth days! That's longer than my year, which is 225 days. You can see how mixed up I am as I rotate east to west, just the opposite of the Earth. You can see that I can't celebrate any holidays since my day is longer than my year. I love celebrations so I'll ask the Planet Master to let me become **Mars**.

(Continued)

May be copied for classroom use. *From Get Up and Move with Nonfiction* by Nancy Polette. Westport, CT: Teacher Ideas Press. Copyright © 2008.

Did you know that humans named **Mars**, the god of war after me? You'll find me between Earth and Jupiter. My day is just a bit longer than a day on Earth. Scientists study me for signs of life. They poke at me with satellite cameras. I'd like to be left alone so I will ask the Planet Master to let me become **Jupiter.** Jupiter is too far away for cameras to reach.

Boy, am I cold! My name is **Jupiter** and the closest I come to the sun is 460 million miles. It takes me 12 years to go around the sun one time. One day on me lasts ten hours compared to the Earth's 24 hours. I am tired all the time since I get only a few hours of sleep each five hour night. I'd really be happy to be warmer and get more sleep. I'll ask the Planet Master to let me become **Mercury.**

PLANETS: INFORMATION

Mercury is the closest planet to the sun. The orbit, or path, it takes around the sun is not in a circle like Earth. The path it takes is called an ellipse, which is like a circle that has been stretched out. For this reason, the distance from Mercury to the Sun varies from about 27 million miles at its closest, to about 41 million miles at its furthest. Mercury races around the Sun faster than any other planet. A Mercurian year—the time it takes for the planet to go once around the Sun—is only 88 Earth days, while a year on Earth is 365 days. Mercury does not spin as fast as Earth, though, so a Mercurian day—the time it takes a planet to rotate once—is 59 Earth days!

Venus is the second planet from the Sun, located in between Mercury and Earth. The orbit, or path, Venus follows around the Sun is nearly circular, so the planet's distance from the Sun averages about 65 million miles. Being closer to the Sun, a Venusian year—the time it takes for it to complete a trip around the Sun—is just 225 Earth days. Venus spins more slowly than Earth, though, so a day on Venus—the time it takes for the planet to turn once—is 243 Earth days, which means that a day on Venus is longer than its year! Even more strange is the fact that Venus rotates from east to west, which is just the opposite of Earth and most of the other planets.

Mars is the fourth planet from the Sun, located in between Earth and Jupiter. Mars is much further away from the Sun than Earth, with an average distance of around 140 million miles. The orbit, or path, the planet takes around the Sun is a mild ellipse, or stretched circle, with Mars being about 128 million miles from the Sun at its closest and 154 million miles away at its furthest. Since Mars is so much further away from the Sun than Earth, a Martian year—the time it takes to go around the Sun once—is much longer, at 687 Earth days. A Martian day—the time it takes the planet to spin around once—is a little longer than an Earth day, at 24 hours and 37 minutes.

Jupiter is the fifth planet from the Sun, located in between Mars and Saturn. Jupiter is the first gas planet in our solar system, as well as being the first of what are called the Outer Planets. Jupiter is much further away from the Sun than Earth. Its average distance from the Sun is almost 470 million miles. Its orbit, or path, around the sun is nearly a perfect circle. The closest it comes to the sun is about 460 million miles, and the furthest away it gets is a little over 500 million miles. Since Jupiter is so much further away from the Sun than Earth, its year—the time it takes to go around the sun once—is very long. A year on Jupiter is almost 12 Earth years! A day on Jupiter—the amount of time it takes to spin around once—is much shorter than a day here on Earth. The giant planet's day is only about 10 hours long, less than half as long as an Earth day.

Good Reading: *Messages from Mars* by Loreen Leedy and Andrew Schuerger. Holiday House, 2006.

GOOD READING: ASTRONOMY

Atkins, Jeannine. *Wings and Rockets.* Farrar, 2003.
    The story of women in air and space.

Berger, Melvin and Gilda. *Do Stars Have Points?* Scholastic, 2007
    Frequently asked questions about the universe are answered in easy-to-read text.

Branley, Franklyn. *Planets in Our Solar System.* HarperCollins, 1998.
    Clear explanation and description of each planet.

Croswell, Ken. *See the Stars.* Boyds Mill, 2005.
    An explanation of the twelve best and brightest star patterns in the night sky, one for each month.

Davis, Kenneth. *Don't Know Much About Space?* HarperCollins, 2001.
    Fascinating facts presented in an easy-to-read format.

Dyson, Marianne. *Space Station Science.* Scholastic, 1999.
    An explanation of all the systems needed to keep the International Space Station up and running, including space experiments, space travel, and space stations of the future.

Hillard, Richard. *Neil, Buzz and Mike Go to the Moon.* Boyds Mill, 2005.
    The story of *Apollo* 11 and the three men who made the historic flight to the moon.

Kingfisher Young People's Series. *Young People's Book of Space.* Kingfisher, 2005
    An award-winning series with clear descriptions and full color illustrations.

Oppenheim, Shulamith. *What Is the Full Moon Full Of?* Boyds Mill, 2005.
    A boy and his grandmother stroll through the woods wondering what the full moon is full of.

Rathbun, Elizabeth. *Exploring Your Solar System.* National Geographic, 1989.
    A guided tour of the nine planets, the Milky Way, and comets.

Simon, Seymour. *Galaxies.* Morrow, 1998.
    A step-by-step introduction to, and description of, the many galaxies in the universe.

ANIMAL CIRCLE STORY

Be sure to tell where it lives, what it eats, what it looks like, and what it does.

The **Bengal Tiger** is a large, striped cat from India, Bangladesh, Nepal, Bhutan, and Burma. It lives in a variety of habitats, including rainforests and dense grasslands. It can live to about 18 years in captivity, and probably a few years less in the wild. Bengal tigers are mostly solitary, but sometimes travel in groups of 3 or 4. Male Bengal tigers are up to 10 feet long; females are up to 9 feet long. The tail is about 3 feet long. The fur is usually orange-brown with black stripes. The fur on the belly is white with black stripes. White Bengal tigers (with white fur and black stripes) are very rare. Tigers have long, sharp teeth in powerful jaws. The Bengal tiger is a carnivore (meat-eater). The tiger often kills its prey with a bite on the neck. It eats deer, pigs, antelopes, cattle, young elephants, and buffalo.

Leopards are wild cats that live in rainforests, woodlands, plains, deserts, and shrubby areas. They are found in Africa, the Middle East, parts of China, India, Siberia, and Southeast Asia. Leopards are fast runners, good swimmers, and excellent tree climbers. They often hide their food in trees. The leopard's call sounds like a raspy cough, not a roar. Leopards live up to 21 years in captivity. These graceful, medium-sized cats grow to be about 3.5-5.5 feet long; the tail is 2-3 feet long. Adults weigh from 65 to 175 pounds. Males are larger than females. Some leopards have dark rosettes on a black background, making them appear black; these leopards are called black panthers. Cubs are gray when they are born.

The **Asian Elephant** is a huge land animal that lives in India, Malaysia, Sumatra, and Sri Lanka. This elephant is used extensively for labor. Its life span is up to 70 years. It lives in family groups headed by a female (called a cow). Elephants are excellent swimmers. Asian elephants average about 8 feet tall at the shoulder. Males weigh up to 6 tons. Only males have tusks (large, pointed ivory teeth). They have very thick, wrinkled, gray-brown skin that is almost hairless. Elephants breathe through two nostrils at the end of their trunk. The trunk is also used to get water and food. Elephants eat roots, grasses, leaves, bark, bananas, and sugar cane.

Camels are large mammals that live in dry areas. The Arabian camels are found in the very hot deserts of North Africa and the Middle East. Bactrian camels are found in the rocky deserts and steppes of Asia that get very hot and very cold. The camel's hump contains fat (and NOT water). The camel can go without food and water for 3 to 4 days. It is well adapted to desert life. Camels are very strong mammals with wide, padded feet. They have thick, leathery pads on their knees and chest. Bushy eyebrows and two rows of long eyelashes protect their eyes from sand. Their mouth is extremely tough, allowing camels to eat thorny desert plants. Camels are over 7 feet tall at the hump and weigh in excess of 1,600 pounds. Camels are plant-eaters.

Good Reference: *Encyclopedia of Animals* by Richard Beatty. Dorling Kindersley, 2005.

MOVING LIKE AN ANIMAL

Number of Players: Four or more.

Objective: Students will identify an animal by watching a player move like the animal.

Procedure: Pick a variety of animals. Write each animal name on a separate note card. Put all the cards in a container. Players form a circle and each picks a card. While music is playing, players enter the circle one by one. The player in the circle demonstrates how the animal moves. Other players get three guesses. The player with the correct guess is next in the circle. If no guesses are correct, the player states his/her animal and chooses someone to take his/her place in the center of the circle.

Follow Up: Introduce books on how animals move.

Suggested names for animal cards

lion	elephant	python	skunk
dog	cat	pig	chicken
rabbit	squirrel	turtle	fox
deer	horse	kangaroo	hawk

GOOD READING: ANIMALS

Bishop, Nic. *The Secrets of Animal Flight.* Houghton Mifflin, 2007.
Engaging text and stop-action photography show how animals fly.

Dewey, Jennifer. *Wildlife Rescue.* Boyds Mill, 2001.
The story of Dr. Kathleen Ramsay's wildlife center in New Mexico.

Hatkoff, Isabella, et al. *Owen and Mzee: The Language of Friendship.* Scholastic, 2007.
The true story of a young hippo lost after the terrible tsunami in Southeast Asia who adopted a 120-year-old tortoise as his mother.

Heard, Georgia. *Creatures of Earth, Sea and Sky.* Boyds Mill, 1992.
Short poems about a variety of wild animals.

Llewellyn, Claire. *Ask Dr. K. Fisher About Animals.* Kingfisher Books, 2007.
Answers the problems that plague wild creatures about themselves, their peers, and family life. Amusing and informative.

Quinlan, Susan E. *The Case of the Monkeys That Fell from the Trees.* Boyds Mill, 2003.
Eleven ecological mysteries reveal why tropical forests are so fascinating and fragile.

Ryder, Joanne. Just For A Day Series. *White Bear, Ice Bear*; *Winter Whale*; and *Jaguar in the Rain Forest.* William Morrow, 1990.
A child magically becomes a wild creature and experiences the creature's life for one day.

Schwartz, David M. *If You Hopped Like a Frog.* Scholastic, 1999.
"If you hopped like a frog you could jump from home plate to first base in one mighty leap." A fun comparison of animal and human abilities.

Swinburne, Stephen. *Moon in Bear's Eyes.* Boyd's Mill, 2005.
Mother bear emerges from hibernation and teaches her cubs to forage for food and defend their finds.

Wilkes, Angela. *Animal Homes.* Kingfisher Books, 2007.
Presents different places and spaces that animals choose to call home. Learn to construct animal habitats including a nest and a hamster playpen.

May be copied for classroom use. *From Get Up and Move with Nonfiction* by Nancy Polette. Westport, CT: Teacher Ideas Press. Copyright © 2008.

DINOSAUR CIRCLE STORY

Use the information below and any additional information you may find to create your story. Include: description, location, habits, and diet. Be sure to tell why a dinosaur would want to be transformed into a different dinosaur. Create an imaginary character that would bring the transformation about.

150 million years ago **Allosaurus** was the most common carnivorous dinosaur in Jurassic North America. Allosaurus means "different lizard," named for its unusual vertebrae, lighter than those of other dinosaurs. It ate plant-eating dinosaurs and grew up to 42 feet long, 10 feet tall, and weighed 4.5 tons. Fossils have been found in Colorado, Montana, New Mexico, Oklahoma, South Dakota, Utah, and Wyoming.

Ankylosaurus had to eat a huge amount of low-lying plant material to sustain itself so its gut must have been very large. It probably had a fermentation compartment to aid in the digestion of the tough plant material, producing prodigious amounts of gas! It was 25-45 feet long, 4 feet tall, and weighed 3-4 tons. It lived 70-65 million years ago. Ankylosaurus fossils have been found in the western United States (Montana) and Canada (Alberta).

Diplodocus, which means "double-beamed," lived 150 million years ago. Its main food was probably conifers, which were the dominant plant when the large sauropods lived. Secondary food sources may have included ginkgos, seed ferns, cycads, ferns, club mosses, and horsetails. Diplodocus had blunt teeth (but only in the front of the jaws), useful for stripping foliage (leaves). It was about 90 feet long, 16 feet tall, and weighed 10-20 tons. Many Diplodocus fossils have been found in the Rocky Mountains of the western United States (in Colorado, Montana, Utah, and Wyoming).

Iguanodon means "Iguana tooth." Iguanodon probably ate cycads, conifers, and ginkgos. It was 20-30 feet long, 9 feet tall, and weighed 4-5 tons. It lived 135-125 million years ago Fossils have been found in Europe (in England, Belgium, and Germany), northern Africa, and the United States.

Follow Up: Introduce books about dinosaurs.

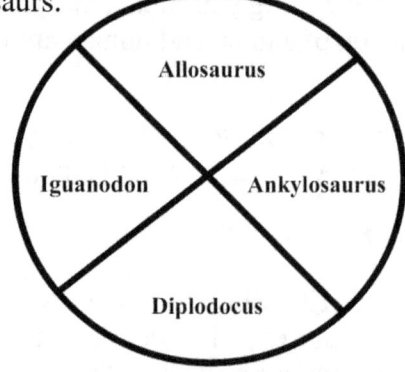

Good Reading: *Raptor: The Life of a Young Deinonychus* by Michael Henry. Abrams, 2007.

WHAT WAS IT? PREHISTORIC CREATURES

Number of Players: Three

Objective: To give a clear description of a setting and of a creature found in that setting.

Procedure: Two players read one of the descriptions below of meeting a prehistoric creature. When the reading is finished, they take the parts of the observers and create a dialogue to describe where they were and what they saw. The third person takes the part of a questioner and can interrupt with a question at any time. The players must answer every question asked. At the end of the dialogue the audience must try to guess the setting and the creature.

150 million years ago **Allosaurus** was the most common meat-eating dinosaur in North America. It often ate other smaller dinosaurs. Allosaurus means "different lizard," named for its unusual vertebrae, lighter than those of other dinosaurs. Half of its body was its tail. It had very sharp claws and teeth and its front legs were smaller than its back legs. It ate plant-eating dinosaurs and grew up to 42 feet long, 10 feet tall, and weighed 4.5 tons. Fossils have been found in Colorado, Montana, New Mexico, Oklahoma, South Dakota, Utah, and Wyoming.

Ankylosaurus had to eat a huge amount of low-lying plant material to sustain itself so its gut must have been very large. It probably had a fermentation compartment to aid in the digestion of the tough plant material, producing prodigious amounts of gas! It was 25-45 feet long, 4 feet tall, and weighed 3-4 tons. It is easy to recognize since it is wider than it is long with short, squat legs and rows of bony spikes along its back. Its long tail ends in a thick club. It lived 70-65 million years ago. Ankylosaurus fossils have been found in the western United States (Montana) and Canada (Alberta).

Diplodocus, which means "double-beamed," lived 150 million years ago. Its main food was probably conifers, which were the dominant plant when the large sauropods lived. Secondary food sources may have included ginkgos, seed ferns, cycads, ferns, club mosses, and horsetails. Diplodocus had a small head, a very long neck, and a long tail. It had blunt teeth (but only in the front of the jaws), useful for stripping foliage (leaves). It was able to rear up on its hind legs to eat high vegetation. It was about 90 feet long, 16 feet tall, and weighed 10-20 tons. Many Diplodocus fossils have been found in the Rocky Mountains of the western United States (in Colorado, Montana, Utah, and Wyoming).

Good Reading: *Dinosaur Discoveries* by Gail Gibbons. Holiday House, 2005; *Raptor, The Life of a Young Deinonychus* by Michel Henry. Abrams, 2007

GOOD READING: PREHISTORIC CREATURES

Dixon, Dougal. *Dougal Dixon's Amazing Dinosaurs: The Fiercest, The Tallest, The Toughest and The Smallest.* Boyds Mill, 2000.
Full color illustrations and diagrams with bite-sized pieces of dinosaur information.

Dixon, Dougal. *Dougal Dixon's Dinosaurs.* Boyds Mill, 1998.
A full color collection of dinosaurs with easy-to-read text.

Henry, Michel. *Raptor: The Life of a Young Deinonychus.* Abrams, 2007.
Follow one raptor as he makes his way through the trials of a savage life.

Kerley, Barbara. *The Dinosaurs of Waterhouse Watkins.* Scholastic, 2001.
The true story of a Victorian artist who brought dinosaurs to life through his drawings and models.

Kumin, Maxine. *Mites to Mastodons.* Houghton Mifflin, 2006.
Poems about a wide variety of animals including those that are extinct.

Lessem, Don. *Dinosaur Worlds: New Dinosaurs, New Discoveries.* Boyds Mill, 1996.
Reconstructions of sixteen prehistoric habitats and examination of fossil evidence tell the story of the dinosaurs rise and fall.

Lessem, Don. *Dinosaurs to Dodos.* Scholastic, 1999.
An encyclopedia of extinct animals including causes of their extinction, and the modern discoveries that are now revealing their lost worlds.

Myers, Jack. *What Happened to the Mammoths?* Boyds Mill, 2000.
Twelve explorations into the animal world answer a host of questions about the origins and habits of many creatures.

Pringle, Laurence. *Dinosaurs! Strange and Wonderful.* Boyds Mill, 1995.
Dramatic, accurate illustrations accompany basic facts about dinosaurs.

Scholastic Reader Collection. *Dinosaurs*; *What the Dinosaurs Saw*; and *Dinosaur Garden.* Scholastic, 2007.
Readers are introduced to fossils and different species of dinosaurs through informative, funny, and even frightening tales.

BE AN INVENTOR

Number of Players: Six

Objective: To explore the concept of invention by creating a machine that does not exist.

Directions: The players will be given one of the cards below. Without prior discussion, one player starts a repetitive activity and a noise to accompany the activity. In turn, each player adds to the machine with appropriate noise and activity. The machine can be sped up or slowed down but must, in some way, achieve the intended objective.

Follow Up: Introduce a variety of books on inventions and inventors.

A machine that will water plants when the home owner is on vacation.
A machine that will automatically wipe up spills on the floor.
A window washer for hard to reach windows.
A bird feeder that will distribute just the right amount of seed.
A machine that will fold and put away clothes.

Good Reading: *Blunder or Brainstorm: Fact and Fiction of Inventors and Inventions* by Nancy Polette. Pieces of Learning, 2006.

GOOD ADVICE

Number of Players: Two teams of four.

Objective: To learn about four or more inventors and their inventions and to rank order their contributions to mankind.

Procedure: Each team member will choose a card and share the information on the card with other team members. The team will then make a list of four criteria to determine the usefulness of an invention to mankind. The team will apply the criteria to the work of the inventors on their cards and rank order the four inventions from most to least important, giving reasons for their ranking.

Louis Bleriot (1872-1936) Used the money he made from developing the automobile search light to building monoplanes. He was the first to cross the English Channel in a heavier-than-air machine.	*Johann Gutenberg (1397-1468)* German printer who invented movable type, which resulted in the first printing press that allowed multiple pages to be printed. Books no longer had to be written or copied by hand.
Gail Borden Jr. (1801-1874) An American dairyman and surveyor who laid out the city of Galveston for Stephen Austin. He developed a process for evaporating milk so pioneers and housewives would not have to worry about milk spoiling.	*Lee DeForest (1873-1961)* He was a pioneer in the development of wireless telegraphy, sound pictures, and television. His triode enabled sound to travel coast to coast without wires. He is frequently called "the father of radio."
Moses Farmer (1820-1893) In 1847 he exhibited an electric train that carried children and in 1851 in Boston, installed the first electric fire alarm in any city. Twenty years before Edison, he produced electric lamps.	*George Eastman (1854-1932)* By his many photographic inventions he brought about photography as a popular hobby. He developed the dry plate process, roll film and the Kodak camera, as well as the process for color photography.
Cornelius Drebbel (1572-1634) Dutch inventor who developed an atmospherically-driven clock, and the first navigable submarine. Its first voyage was made in 1620.	*Edmund Cartwright (1743-1823)* The inventor of the power loom, the parent of the modern loom, which was the first machine to make practical the weaving of wide cotton cloth.

Good Reading: *Blunder or Brainstorm: Fact and Fiction of Inventors and Inventions* by Nancy Polette. Pieces of Learning, 2006.

TITLE STORIES: SCIENCE

Players: Teams of five or six.

Objective: Students will create a title and story using words from other titles.

Procedure: Select teams of five or six players. Each team receives a list of six science titles. One word is to be chosen from four to six of the titles. The words are put together to form a new title. The form or tense of a word can be changed. The team then creates and tells a story related to the new title. The story should contain at least three science facts. See science titles on the following pages.

Example:

The Story About Human Evolution

Nuclear Energy, Past **of** Trouble

What Has Ten Legs and **a** body?

How To Be a Nature Detective

The **Spider** Webs We See

Wheels at Work

A Dinosaur Has a **Colorful** Past

Words Chosen
The
Story
of
a
Colorful
Spider

THE STORY OF A COLORFUL SPIDER

In a small town in Italy there lived an old woman who had lost her husband many years earlier. Every day she wore a long black dress and black hat with a red rose on top. She never spoke to anyone. She never had visitors. Her pets were small spiders who lived in every corner of her humble house. She caught flies for her spiders. She sang to her spiders as they wove their webs. She made sure the house was not too hot or too cold. The spiders loved the old woman and she loved them.

One cold winter day the old woman did not get out of bed. The spiders crawled around her to see what was the matter. The old woman was dead. The spiders called upon the spider king to make magic. He could not bring the old woman back to life, but he wove a web over all of her pets and turned them black with red spots on their bellies. From that day on, when people saw the spiders they called them Black Widows, and just as they had with the old woman, they left the spiders alone.

SCIENCE TITLES

Earth Keepers
Bones, Bones, Dinosaur Bones
To the Top of the World
Flash, Crash, Rumble and Roll
Operation Grizzly Bear
Science Experiments You Can Eat
Why Can't You Unscramble an Egg?
Under the Ground
Frozen Man
Journey to the Planets
Life and Times of the Honeybee

MORE SCIENCE TITLES

The Science Book of Motion
Dinosaurs Down Under
All About Alligators
Animal Perception and Communication
A Photographic Story of Hatching
Chemically Active
Stories Science Photos Tell
Come Back Salmon
Great Northern Diver: The Loon
What Does the Crow Know?
Two Eyes, a Nose and a Mouth

THE ADDED PHRASE SCIENCE REPORT

Number of Players: Two

Procedure: Each member of the audience writes a short 3-5 word phrase on a slip of paper. Phrases are placed face down on the floor or a desk. Two players, taking the parts of two scientists begin a dialogue giving facts about the science topic they have chosen to study. Any science topic of interest can be used.

As the dialogue progresses, each player must pick up one of the slips of paper and use the phrase in his or her dialogue. The phrase must make sense given the context of the subject area. The game ends when each player has used four of the phases.

Follow Up: Introduce books on one or more of the topics that follow.

Sample Topics:

Mountains
Discuss how mountains are formed, why so few creatures live high in the mountains, and why they are one of the world's most challenging habitats.
See: *Mountains* by Margaret Hynes. Kingfisher Books, 2007.

Fossils
Discuss how fossils are formed. What is a fossil? How can scientists determine the age of a fossil?
See: *The Best Book of Fossils, Rocks and Minerals* by Chris Pellant. Kingfisher Books, 2007.

Sea Turtles
Where does the female turtle lay her eggs? What predators search for and eat the eggs? What happens when the surviving eggs hatch? How do the hatchlings survive? How do they make it to the sea?
See: *Turtle Tide* by Stephen R. Swinburne. Boyds Mill, 2005.

Space Travel
Players can take the parts of Neil Armstrong and Buzz Aldrin to talk about their trip to the moon: how they prepared for the mission, any problems encountered, the trip itself, and what they found when they got there.
See: *Neil, Buzz and Mike Go to the Moon* by Richard Hilliard. Boyds Mill, 2005.

Animal Myths
Discuss how the following animal myths are not true: Bats are blind. Camels store water in their humps. Ostriches hide their heads in the sand. Owls are wise. Bulls charge when they see red.
See: *Animal Fact, Animal Fable* by Seymour Simon. Crown, 1979.

May be copied for classroom use. *From Get Up and Move with Nonfiction* by Nancy Polette. Westport, CT: Teacher Ideas Press. Copyright © 2008.

THE ADDED PHRASE SCIENCE REPORT: MORE SAMPLE TOPICS

Alike and Different
　　Discuss the differences in these animal pairs: Sheep and goats. Donkeys and mules. Rats and mice. Kangaroos and wallabies. Crocodiles and alligators. Butterflies and moths. Frogs and toads.
　　See: *Animal Wonders* by John Wexo. Wildlife Education, 1998.

Environment
　　Discuss one or more of the following: Earth Day. The Clean Air Act. The Environmental Protection Agency. The Endangered Species Act. The Safe Drinking Water Act. The Toxic Substance Control Act. The Earth's ozone layer. Global warming. The Greenhouse Effect.
　　See: *Earthday: Keeping Our Planet Clean* by Elaine Landau. Enslow, 2002.

Endangered Species
　　Discuss the reasons for and efforts to reverse the dwindling populations of: Hawaii's native bird species. Endangered fish. Mountain gorillas. The endangered rhinoceros. The elephant. The American Eagle.
　　See: *Endangered Animals* by John Wexo. Wildlife Education, 2001.

Inventors
　　Discuss the life and work of one of the following inventors: Guglielmo Marconi, Thomas Edison, Alexander Graham Bell, Elijah Otis, or Benjamin Franklin.
　　See: *Invention* by Lionel Bender. DK Publishers, 2005.

Planets and Space
　　Discuss the size and position of the planets from the sun. How craters were formed on Mercury. The voyage of *Mariner* 10. The Earth's orbit around the sun. The surface of the moon and the first moonwalk by astronauts. A trip to Mars: how long it would take and what you would find there. The effect of the lack of gravity in space.
　　See: *Planets* by Carol Rybeck. Gareth Stevens, 2006.

Sea Life
　　Discuss the unusual characteristics of one or more of these ocean creatures: electric eels, sharks, blue whale, ocean sunfish, flashlight fish, lungfish, arapaima, or starfish.
　　See: *Sea Critters* by Sylvia Earle. National Geographic, 2000.

WHAT COLOR IS IT?

Science: The Experiment

Number of Players: Four to six.

Objective: To give a vivid description of a setting by adding adjectives.

Procedure: Each player in turn will read a sentence strip adding as many color words as possible. Sentences are from *Dr. Jekyll and Mr. Hyde* by Robert Louis Stevenson.

Follow Up: Introduce books on science experiments.

I entered my laboratory and closed the door, knowing well that I risked death.
I picked up the flask and looked at the liquid. I drew the curtains to keep my experiment from prying eyes.
The temptation of a discovery overcame my doubts. From a shelf I took three bottles.
The first bottle contained a liquid I had purchased from a firm of chemists.
I mixed in a quantity of a salt which I knew, from my experiments, to be the next ingredient required.
I compounded the elements, watched them boil and smoke together in the glass.
I poured the potion into a glass, sat in my chair, stared for a time at the walls and then drank.
I felt a grinding in the bones and saw colors whirl around the room. My face turned an awful color and I collapsed on the rug.

Extension Activity

Two players take turns describing your classroom or the science laboratory in alternate sentences using as many color words as they can.

READERS THEATRE: LUTHER BURBANK

Number of Players: Four

Objective: To use critical listening skills in learning about the life of a famous scientist.

Directions: Three players read the parts of the scientist. One player taking the part of the host asks questions. Only one scientist must give completely truthful answers. The audience listens critically to determine who the real scientist is.

Follow Up: Introduce biographies of famous scientists including Luther Burbank.

Reading Parts: Host, Luther Burbank #1, Luther Burbank #2, Luther Burbank #3

Host: Welcome everyone to "Which Scientist Is It?" Three of our guests are pretending to be the famous plant wizard, Luther Burbank. Only one is telling the complete truth about himself. It is up to you to decide which scientist is the real Luther Burbank. Now, let's meet our guests.

Host: Would you tell us your name and something about your early life.

Burbank #1: I was born in Lancaster, Massachusetts in 1849. I was the thirteenth of fifteen children and to feed the family my mother kept a large garden, which was a delight to me in my early years.

Burbank #2: I was born in Lancaster, Massachusetts in 1849. I came from a large family and my formal education ended with elementary school. My father died when I was 21 years old and left me a small amount of money, which I used to buy seventeen acres of land.

Burbank #3: I was born in Lancaster, Massachusetts in 1849. Being from a large family I had very little education but spent a lot of time with plants, which fascinated me, in my mother's large garden.

Host: Tell us about your interest in plant life.

Burbank #1: Plants always fascinated me and I got most of my education about them by watching gardening shows on television. I tried cross breeding plants and developed the popular Burbank potato in 1874.

Burbank #2: Some say I am not really a scientist because I did not keep the careful records expected in scientific research. Never the less, I developed over 800 varieties of plants during my 55-year career.

Burbank #3: After I graduated from college I went to Santa Rosa, California where I purchased four acres of land and began my experiments. It was here that I developed the Shasta Daisy.

Host: Which of your experiments gives you the most pride?

Burbank #1: It is hard to say. I think the ranchers out West would say that the spineless cactus is the greatest plant development. Cattle could not eat cactus with spines, but today the spineless cactus provides an additional source of food for them

Burbank #2: I take greatest pride in the Burbank potato, which is large and brown-skinned with white flesh. It has become the world's most prominent potato and is the potato used for McDonalds' french fries.

Burbank #3: It would be hard to choose one of the 800 varieties I developed as the most important. More important to me is having a close partnership with nature, helping her to produce new foods for mankind that were never known before.

Host: Now it is time to guess which is the real Luther Burbank. We will vote by a show of hands. Is it #1? Is it #2? Is it #3? Now, will the real Luther Burbank step forward.

Answer: #2

Good Reading: *Some Plants Have Funny Names* by Diana Cross. Crown, 1983.

READERS THEATRE: MARIA MITCHELL

Number of Players: Four

Objective: To use critical listening skills in learning about the life of a famous scientist.

Directions: Three players read the parts of the scientist. One player taking the part of the host asks questions. Only one scientist must give completely truthful answers. The audience listens critically to determine who the real scientist is.

Follow up: Introduce books on astronomy including biographies of Maria Mitchell.

Reading Parts: Host, Maria Mitchell #1, Maria Mitchell #2, Maria Mitchell #3

Host: Welcome everyone to "Which Scientist Is It?" Three of our guests are pretending to be the famous astronomer, Maria Mitchell. Only one is telling the complete truth about herself. It is up to you to decide which scientist is the real Maria Mitchell. Now let's meet our guests.

Host: Would you tell us your name and something about your early life?

Maria Mitchell #1: I was born in 1818 of Quaker parents who, surprisingly, made sure that I received the same education that boys of that time received. I was an excellent student and had an early interest in astronomy.

Maria Mitchell #2: I was born in 1818, was well-educated and worked for a time as a librarian. My father was a man of science and was pleased when I wanted to spend time at his observatory.

Maria Mitchell #3: In the early 1800s it was unusual for a girl to get the same education as boys of the time, but my parents made sure I was well-educated. I spent many hours in my scientist father's observatory and was fascinated from an early age with astronomy.

Host: Will you tell us of your early discoveries.

Maria Mitchell #1: I was not a very good student but did spend lots of time in my father's observatory. I was twenty-nine years old when I discovered what was later named "Miss Mitchell's Comet." In 1848 I received a prize for my discovery from King Frederick VII.

Maria Mitchell #2: As a young woman I spent every spare minute I had in my father's observatory making notes about the things I saw through his telescope. My father thought I was a nuisance and chased me off every time he found me there. Never the less, for my discovery of the comet I was the first woman to become a member of the American Academy of Arts and Sciences.

Maria Mitchell #3: I later became a professor of astronomy at Vassar College and Director of the Vassar College Observatory.

Host: Has fame changed you in any way?

Maria Mitchell #1: I don't think so. I always enjoyed my college teaching career and in addition fought for the rights of women by co-founding, with Elizabeth Cady Stanton, the American Association for the Advancement of Women.

Maria Mitchell #2: Fame has perhaps made me bold. In protest against slavery I stopped wearing cotton clothing and spoke out strongly against such an inhumane institution.

Maria Mitchell #3: When I found that, despite my reputation and experience, my salary at Vassar was less than younger male professors, I insisted on a salary increase and got it.

Host: Now it is time to guess which is the real Maria Mitchell. We will vote by a show of hands. Is it #1? Is it #2? Is it #3? Now, will the real Maria Mitchell step forward.

Answer: #3

Good Reading: *Mysteries of the Universe* by Franklyn M. Branley. Morrow, 1994

READERS THEATRE: JONAS SALK

Number of Players: Four

Objective: To use critical listening skills in learning about the life of a famous scientist.

Directions: Three players read the parts of the scientist. One player taking the part of the host asks questions. Only one scientist must give completely truthful answers. The audience listens critically to determine who the real scientist is.

Follow up: Introduce biographies of those responsible for medical discoveries.

Reading Parts: Host, Jonas Salk #1, Jonas Salk #2, Jonas Salk #3

Host: Welcome everyone to "Which Scientist Is It?" Three of our guests are pretending to be the famous scientist, Jonas Salk. Only one is telling the complete truth about himself. It is up to you to decide which scientist is the real Jonas Salk. Now let's meet our guests.

Host: Please introduce yourselves to our audience.

Jonas Salk #1: My name is Jonas Salk. I was born in New York City in 1914, the son of immigrant parents. My parents had little money and very little education, but were determined that their children would do better in life than they had. They knew education was the key to success.

Jonas Salk #2: My name is Jonas Salk. I was born in New York City in 1914. I had little time for games as a child since my parents insisted that a good education was essential and expected me to study hard. They wanted me to become a lawyer.

Jonas Salk #3: My name is Jonas Salk. I was born in New York City in 1914, After years of hard study I graduated from high school and entered City College of New York. I intended to study law but after seeing several medical shows on television I decided to become a doctor.

Host: How did you become interested in research?

Jonas Salk #1: While in medical school I spent a year studying the flu virus. This led to the development of the vaccine that prevented many deaths from the flu. There was no recurrence of the flu epidemic of World War I.

Jonas Salk #2: When I was born in 1950 many children were infected with the virus that causes polio. After working with the flu virus I knew it would be possible to develop a vaccine against polio. It took me eight years, but I did it.

Jonas Salk #3: In 1947 I accepted an appointment to the University of Pittsburgh Medical School. I spent the next eight years working to develop a vaccine to prevent polio. The vaccine I developed was a killed virus and proved to be very effective in preventing polio.

Host: How did you deal with the fame from your discovery?

Jonas Salk #1: I refused to patent the vaccine. I had no desire for personal profit. I just wished to see the vaccine distributed as widely as possible.

Jonas Salk #2: My vaccine required an injection and I was somewhat concerned when a few years after my discovery an oral, live virus vaccine was put on the market. Tragically, some patients contracted polio from the live vaccine.

Jonas Salk #3: In my later years I founded the Jonas Salk Institute for Biological Studies. I continued research into the AIDS virus and published several books. My sons, who are both medical scientists, will carry on my work,

Host: Now it is time to guess which is the real Jonas Salk. We will vote by a show of hands. Is it #1? Is it #2? Is it #3? Now, will the real Jonas Salk step forward.

Answer: #1

Good Reading: *Jonas Salk* by Don McLeese. Rourke, 2006.

READERS THEATRE OUTLINE

Create Your Own Famous Scientist Readers Theatre

Reading Parts: Host, _____ #1, _____ #2, _____ #3

Host: Welcome everyone to "Which Scientist Is It?" Three of our guests are pretending to be the famous scientist, _____. Only one is telling the complete truth about himself/herself. It is up to you to decide which scientist is telling the real _____. Now, let's meet our guests.

Host: Tell us when and where you were born and something about your early life.

_____ **#1:** _____
_____
_____
_____
_____
_____
_____
_____

_____ **#2:** _____
_____
_____
_____
_____
_____
_____
_____

_____ **#3:** _____
_____
_____
_____
_____
_____
_____
_____

May be copied for classroom use. *From Get Up and Move with Nonfiction* by Nancy Polette. Westport, CT: Teacher Ideas Press. Copyright © 2008.

Host: What were some of the problems or difficulties you had to overcome before making your discovery?

_____ **#1:** _____
_____
_____
_____
_____
_____
_____

_____ **#2:** _____
_____
_____
_____
_____
_____
_____

_____ **#3:** _____
_____
_____
_____
_____
_____
_____

Host: What else would you like our audience to know?

_____ **#1:** _____
_____
_____
_____
_____
_____

_____ #2: _____
_____
_____
_____
_____
_____
_____
_____

_____ #3: _____
_____
_____
_____
_____
_____
_____
_____

Host: Now it is time to guess which scientist is the real _____. We will vote by a show of hands. Is it #1? Is it #2? Is it #3? Now, will the real _____ step forward.

Part Two

Mathematics

There once was a king who knew he could solve any problem in the world until one day . . . [continue the story using as many mathematical terms as possible]

WARM UP GAMES

Number of Players: Circles of eight.

Objective: To quickly recall basic math facts.

Procedure: Each circle selects a person to be the starter. Responses are given clockwise around the circle. If a response is incorrect, the starter must begin again. The circle that completes the given task first is the winner.

A Circle Supervisor states the task to be accomplished and says "Ready, Set, Go!"

Tasks

Count to 200 by fives.

Count to 60 by fours.

Count to 192 by twelves.

Count to 180 by threes.

Any other task can be given.

Variation

A line of five players presents a math problem. The audience must give the answer.

Example:

Player one gives a number (15)

Player two says plus, minus, times, or divided by

Player three gives a number (4)

Player four says plus, minus, times, or divided by

Player five gives a number (10)

All players say "EQUALS"

The audience gives the answer: _____

WHAT'S YOUR EXCUSE?

Number of Players: Teams of three.

Objective: To display an understanding of math vocabulary by encoding it in a new way. (Any other math vocabulary can be substituted.)

Procedure: Each team will choose one row of words, across, down, or diagonally. The team will create an excuse using all of the words in the row correctly

Example: What excuse can you give as to why the 1,500 mile long Great Wall of China was never finished?

acre	adjacent	altitude	complex	sector	billion
bisect	calculate	Celsius	century	closure	comparison
axis	maximum	formula	decrease	diagram	terminate
decade	dimension	deposit	diagonal	division	equality
error	expanded	reduce	exponent	exterior	face value
data	interval	integer	cubed	substitute	tally

Good Reading: *Math Curse* by Jon Scieszka, Viking, 1995.

IT'S ALL IN A WORD

Number of Players: One

Objective: The student will associate unlike items to develop a monologue.

Procedure: The player will choose any three items in a row and use the three items to explain how to build a better mouse trap or why he/she had difficulty in solving a math problem. Use for any math vocabulary.

How to Build a Better Mouse Trap.

polygon	measurement	parallel
negative number	add	subtract
multiply	divide	decimal

Why Couldn't You Solve the Problem?

acute angle	baker's dozen	calculate
common denominator	face value	improper fraction
perfect number	word problem	meter stick

GEOMETRY MATCH

Number of Players Four teams, four on each team.

Objective: To match geometry words with their definitions.

Procedure: Cut apart the words and their definitions. One team has words; the other, definitions (p. 49). Members must circulate until they find the correct match. The team finding correct matches for its four words first is the winner.

1. circumference	2. circle	3. angle	4. cube
5. horizontal	6. diameter	7. hexagon	8. radius
9. octagon	10. parallel	11. perimeter	12. pie
13. rhombus	14. segment	15. pyramid	16. ray

Good Reading: *Janice Van Cleve's Geometry for Every Kid: Easy Activities that Make Learning Geometry Fun* by Janice VanCleave. Wiley, 1999.

DEFINITIONS FOR GEOMETRY MATCH

A. the regular solid of six equal square sides
B. the length of a straight line through the center of an object
C. the boundary of a closed plane figure
D. perimeter of a circle
E. a polygon of six angles and six sides
F. a closed curve, every point equidistant from a fixed point
G. a plane parallel to the horizon or base line
H. a polygon of eight angles and eight sides
I. a figure formed by two lines extending from the same point
J. a line from the center of a circle to the circumference
K. a polyhedron having for its base a polygon and for faces triangles with a common vertex
L. ratio of the circumference of a circle to its diameter
M. a separate piece of something
N. a parallelogram with four equal sides
O. any of a group of lines diverging from a common center
P. equidistant lines extending in the same direction, not meeting

Answer Key: A-4, B-6, C-11, D-1, E-7, F-2, G-5, H-9, I-3, J-8, K-15, L-12, M-14, N-13, O-16, P-10

May be copied for classroom use. *From Get Up and Move with Nonfiction* by Nancy Polette. Westport, CT: Teacher Ideas Press. Copyright © 2008.

MATH QUOTES

Number of Players: Five to seven, plus a Leader.

Objective: To introduce quotations from mathematicians. The players will create a story two or three lines at a time. Each player will have one slip of paper containing a quotation. The player must work the quotation into the story.

Procedure: The group decides on a good title for a story. Each player in turn, tells the story with two or three sentences, one of which contains the quotation from the slip of paper he or she is holding. Each player, in turn, continues the story in the same way until the story is told. The story should be completed in not less than two or more than three rounds.

The Quotations

"Mathematics is a journey into a strange wilderness."   —*W.S. Anglin*
"There is safety in numbers."   —*Anonymous*
"Things of this world cannot be made known without mathematics."   —*Roger Bacon*
"Life is a school of probability."   —*Walter Bagehot*
" 'Obvious' is the most dangerous word in mathematics."   —*Eric Temple Bell*

Good Reading: Biographies of famous mathematicians.

MORE MATH QUOTATIONS

"What is now proved was once only imagined."   —*Blake*
"Probability is the very guide of life."   —*Bishop Butler*
"You might prove anything by figures."   —*Thomas Carlyle*
"Perfect numbers like perfect men are very rare."   —*Descartes*
"Revolutions never occur in mathematics."   —*Michael Crowe*
"It is a capital mistake to theorize before one has data."   —*A.C. Doyle*
"Everything should be made as simple as possible."   —*Albert Einstein*
"Imagination is more important than knowledge."   —*Albert Einstein*

MATHEMATICIAN MIX-UP

Number of Players: Eight or two teams of eight players.

Objective: To reconstruct the life and work of Albert Einstein by retelling events in the order they happened.

Procedure: Each player receives one of the sentence strips below. Working cooperatively they line up in the correct order to tell events in Einstein's life in the order they happened. The team achieving the correct order first wins.

1. He developed the general theory of relativity.
2. He worked in a patent office in Berlin, continuing his studies in physics without help.
3. After earning a doctorate he became a Professor of Physics at the University of Zurich.
4. He won the Nobel Prize for his work on the photoelectric effect.
5. He did not speak his first word until he was four years old.
6. In 1905 he made important contributions to quantum theory.
7. He failed an examination that would have allowed him to study for a diploma as an electrical engineer.
8. By 1911 he was able to predict how a ray of light from a distant star would appear to be bent slightly, in the direction of the sun.

Good Reading: *Albert Einstein* by Patricia Lakin. Simon & Schuster, 2005.

Answer Key: 5, 7, 2, 3, 6, 8, 1, 4

TITLE STORIES: MATH

Players: Teams of five or six.

Objective: Students will create a title and story using words from other titles.

Procedure: Select teams of five or six players. Each team receives a list of six math titles. One or two words are chosen from each of four to six titles. The words are put together to form a new title. The form or tense of a word can be changed. The team then creates and tells a story related to the new title. The story should contain mathematical terms.

Example:

Sir Cumference and the First Round Table
Marvelous Math: A Book of Poems
One Grain of Rice: A **Mathematical** Folktale
The Coin Counting Book
Red Riding Hood's Math **Adventure**

Words Chosen
Sir Cumference
Marvelous
Mathematical
Adventure

SIR CUMFERENCE'S MARVELOUS MATHEMATICAL ADVENTURE

A beast known as Zoid was terrorizing all the cute little angles who lived on the perimeter of Rightangle city. Sir Cumference (who had a well-rounded personality) arrived with his team to destroy Zoid. He planned to put a hex on Zoid's den but found his hex was missing. "My hex a gone," he cried.

Another team member, Ray D. Us liked to be at the center of things. He set a trap between a Simma tree, which was perfectly balanced on all sides and a Geoma tree, which had different shaped leaves. He was sure he could trap a zoid.

Meanwhile, Al T. Tude dressed as "Super Angle" was "scalene" the Empire Straight Building when he hit Zoid on the toe with a ray from the Trap-A-Zoid kit. Zoid fell into the waiting trap below and was equilaterally dead. All of the little angles in the city rejoiced and Mayor Polly Gon, who was known for talking plane and straight, gave Sir Cumference's team her undying thanks.

Good Reading: *Sir Cumference and the First Round Table* by Cindy Neuschwander. Charlesbridge, 1997,

May be copied for classroom use. *From Get Up and Move with Nonfiction* by Nancy Polette. Westport, CT: Teacher Ideas Press. Copyright © 2008.

MATH TITLES

The Greedy Triangle
Safari Park
Anno's Mysterious Multiplying Jar
On Beyond a Million
An Amazing Math Journey
G is for Googol: A Math Alphabet Book
In Code: A Mathematical Journey
The Number Devil
The Grapes of Math
Mind Stretching Math Riddles
Pigs Will Be Pigs, Fun with Math and Money
Math Games Around the World
Even Steven and Odd Todd

MORE MATH TITLES

Counting Caterpillars and Other Math Poems
Math Trek: Adventures in the Math Zone
Tiger Math: Learning to Graph from a Baby Tiger
See and Spy Counting
One Hundred Angry Ants
How Much Is a Million
The Dot and the Line: A Romance in Lower Mathematics
The Adventures of Penrose, the Mathematical Cat
The Man who Counted
A Collection of Mathematical Adventures
Fractals, Googols and Other Mathematical Tales

SEQUELS TO MATH TALES

Number of Players: Three

About the Tale

Sir Cumference and the First Round Table: A Math Adventure by Cindy Neuschwander, illustrated by Wayne Geehan (Charlesbridge, 1997).

King Arthur, his wife Lady Di of Ameter, and their son, Radius, problem solve to find the right shape for a table that the king uses to discuss matters with his knights. This clever tale of geometry has simple diagrams that reinforce math concepts, including circumference, diameter, and Pi.

Procedure: Each member of the audience writes a short 3-5 word phrase on a slip of paper. Phrases are placed face down on the floor. Three players, taking the parts of King Arthur, his wife, and son must begin a dialogue. They discuss different tables and try to decide on the best one for meeting with the knights.

As the dialogue progresses, each player must pick up one of the slips of paper and use the phrase in his or her dialogue. The phrase must make sense given the context of the situation. The game ends when each player has used three of the phases.

Note: Rather than using phrases from the audience, math quotations can be used for this activity.

Additional Activity

Draw the shape of the table you believe would best meet the king's needs.

Give an oral defense of your choice. Use as many geometric terms as you can in your defense.

Good Reading: *Knights of the Kitchen Table* by Jon Scieszka. Viking, 1991.

MORE SEQUELS TO MATH TALES

Math Curse by Jon Scieszka, illustrated by Lane Smith (Viking, 1995)

The math curse begins on a Monday when a little girl's math teacher tells the class that you can think of almost everything as a math problem. And sure enough, from Tuesday morning through the rest of the day almost every event in this girl's life constitutes a math problem—some real, others wacky! Tuesday night she dreams she is trapped in a room with no doors and windows and must solve math problems for a lifetime. But she frees herself by putting a hole in the wall and jumping out, only to be told the next day by her science teacher that "you can think of almost everything as a science experiment!"

Scenario

Create a dialogue between two players telling each other what events in their day constituted a math problem. Phrases from the audience should be used in the dialogue.

Red Riding Hood's Math Adventure by Lalie Harcourt and Ricki Wortzman (Charlesbridge, 2001).

Red Riding Hood is taking a basket of 12 cookies to Grandma, but along the way she encounters nursery rhyme and fairy tale characters who request some of the goodies. At each character's request for 0, 1, or 2 cookies, Red Riding Hood has to figure out how many cookies she has left for Grandma.

Scenario

Four players take the parts of Red Riding Hood and the three characters she meets in the woods. Each asks for cookies and she can share or not as she wishes. Phrases from the audience should be used in the dialogue. A larger number of cookies and requests for cookies can be used.

THE I HAVE, WHO HAS GAME

ARCHIMEDES

Number of Players: Eight

Objective: To retell a mathematical incident from history.

Directions: Distribute cards to players. The player with the starred card reads the question. Players respond with the correct answer and read their questions. The game continues until all cards are read.

I HAVE: He ran home without his clothes telling of his discovery. *** WHO HAS: Who asked Archimedes to find out if his crown was pure gold?	I HAVE: He knew that the same weight of gold would displace less water than an equal weight of silver. WHO HAS: How did Archimedes prove what he knew?
I HAVE: Emperor of Greece, Hiero II wanted to know if his crown was pure gold. WHO HAS: How did Archimedes feel about Hiero's request?	I HAVE: Archimedes took a bath with items containing equal amounts of gold and silver. WHO HAS: What did Archimedes prove?
I HAVE: Archimedes was perplexed. He did not know what to do. WHO HAS: What did Archimedes know about gold?	I HAVE: Archimedes proved that Hiero's crown contained silver as well as gold. WHO HAS What did Archimedes do when he made this discovery?
I HAVE: Archimedes knew that gold has more weight per volume than silver. WHO HAS: How did Archimedes decide to compare gold and silver?	I HAVE: Archimedes jumped out of the bathtub shouting "Eureka!" WHO HAS: What did he do after jumping out of the tub?

Good Reading: *Archimedes: Father of Mathematics* by Mary Gow. Enslow, 2005.

THE I HAVE, WHO HAS GAME

ADA LOVELACE

Number of Players: Eight

Objective: To retell a mathematical incident from history.

Directions: Distribute cards to players. The player with the starred card reads the question. Players respond with the correct answer and read their questions. The game continues until all cards are read.

Follow up: Share books on the history of computers.

I HAVE: Ada predicted that machines might one day compose and play music and draw pictures. * * * WHO HAS: Ada Lovelace, born in 1815, was the daughter of what famous poet?	I HAVE: Ada met Mr. Babbage who had an idea for a calculating machine. WHO HAS: How did Ada help Mr. Babbage?
I HAVE: Ada Lovelace was the daughter of the famous poet, Lord Byron. WHO HAS: How did Ada's mother feel about poets?	I HAVE: Ada laid out a plan for how a calculating machine might work. WHO HAS: In what year was the first computer program written?
I HAVE: Ada's mother disliked poets. She wanted Ada to be a scientist. WHO HAS: What did Ada study as a child?	I HAVE: Ada Lovelace wrote the first computer program in 1843. WHO HAS What other interests did Ada Lovelace have?
I HAVE: Ada studied and was very good at math and science. WHO HAS: What man did Ada meet who had an idea for a new machine?	I HAVE: Ada was very interested in horses and music. WHO HAS: What did Ada predict before her death in 1852?

Good Reading: *Computers Then and Now* by Rebecca Weber. Compass Point, 2005.

THE I HAVE, WHO HAS GAME

ROBERT GODDARD

Number of Players: Eight

Objective: To retell a mathematical incident from history.

Directions: Distribute cards to players. The player with the starred card reads the question. Players respond with the correct answer and read their questions. The game continues until all cards are read.

I HAVE: There would be no space program today without Robert Goddard's discovery of rockets. *** WHO HAS: What gave Robert Goddard the idea for inventing a rocket?	I HAVE: Robert was 44 when he launched his first successful rocket. WHO HAS: How far did the first successful rocket travel?
I HAVE: Watching firecrackers explode and fly into the air gave Robert Goddard the idea for a rocket. WHO HAS: What did Robert do at age 25?	I HAVE: The first successful rocket traveled 41 feet into the sky. WHO HAS: What did the newspapers say about Robert and his rockets?
I HAVE: At age 25 Robert launched rockets in a field on his aunt's farm. WHO HAS: How successful were Robert's first rockets?	I HAVE: The newspapers said Robert was a foolish dreamer. WHO HAS Why did Robert move to New Mexico?
I HAVE: Robert's first rockets fizzled and the neighbors laughed. WHO HAS: How old was Robert when he launched his first successful rocket?	I HAVE: New Mexico had more open space for experimenting with rockets. There he built rockets that flew faster than sound. WHO HAS: What would we not have today without Robert's discovery of the rocket?

Good Reading: *Robert Goddard* by Don McLeese. Rourke, 2006.

THE I HAVE, WHO HAS GAME

BILL GATES

Number of Players: Eight

Objective: To retell a mathematical incident from history.

Directions: Distribute cards to players. The player with the starred card reads the question. Players respond with the correct answer and read their questions. The game continues until all cards are read.

Follow Up: Share books about Bill Gates and the history of computers.

I HAVE: He would like to find new ways to make the computer more useful. * * * WHO HAS: Where and when was Bill Gates born?	I HAVE: Bill Gates went to Harvard University but left in his junior year. WHO HAS: Why didn't Bill finish college?
I HAVE: Bill Gates was born in Seattle, Washington in 1955. WHO HAS: At what age did he develop his first software program?	I HAVE: Bill did not finish college because he wanted to start his own software company. WHO HAS: What company did Bill start?
I HAVE: Bill Gates developed his first software program at age 13. WHO HAS: What did Bill do in High School?	I HAVE: Bill started the Microsoft Corporation which produced software that other companies needed. WHO HAS: What nickname did many give to Bill Gates.
I HAVE: In High School Bill started a company to sell traffic counting software to local governments. WHO HAS: Did Bill Gates go to college?	I HAVE: Many called him "The Computer King." WHO HAS: What are Bill Gates' goals for the future?

Good Reading: *Bill Gates* by Peter Craig. Enslow, 2003.

A MATH PLAY TO FIGURE OUT AND PERFORM

THE MONEY PIG

Adapted from *The Money Box* by Hans Christian Andersen by Nancy Polette

Directions: A team of six players will read through the play and work out the answers to the math problems. The team will then perform the play including the correct answers that are called for.

Reading Parts: Narrator One, Narrator Two, Rag Doll, Clock, Wagon, Money Pig

Narrator One: SHHH! The moon peeks through a playroom window. One by one, the toys come awake. Rag Doll flops down on the floor. Money Pig sits on a shelf nine feet or (1)_____ yards high.

Narrator Two: Wagon rolls round and round. It takes wagon 12 minutes to go all the way around playroom. Wagon can make (2) _____ trips in 96 minutes.

Narrator One: Clock in the corner goes tick, tock and gives the time as 11:00 P.M. It will still be saying tick tock (3) _____ hours later at seven A.M., when the sun comes up.

Rag Doll: What shall we do for fun?

Wagon: We can go for a ride, riding is always fun.

Clock: We can count the minutes. Counting is always fun. Why, in three hours I can count (4)_____ minutes!

Money Pig: I don't want to play with you, I am too important. I have four ten dollar pieces, six five dollar pieces, twenty-two one dollar pieces, and forty-three pennies. That is a total of (5) $_____. That is enough money to buy **all** the toys I want.

Narrator Two: SO, Money Pig sat on a high shelf. Wagon rolled over the floor. Clock counted thirty-two minutes. Rag Doll sang songs by the door.

Rag Doll: It takes me three minutes to sing a song. I have been singing for a whole hour. I have sung (6)_____ songs. What shall we do now?

Wagon: We can have a race. Races are always fun. My father was the Wagon Racing Champion of the toy world. He went around a three-quarter mile race track in one and one half minutes. That came to (7) _____ of a mile per minute.

Money Pig: I don't want to race with you, I am too important. Soon I will have twice as much money as I have right now. Then I will have (8) $_____. This is enough money to buy all the toys in the toy store.

Narrator One: SO, Money Pig sat on a high shelf. Rag Doll fell down with a thump. Wagon rolled faster and faster and hit the high shelf with a bump!

Narrator Two: The high shelf rocked from side to side. Money Pig rocked from side to side. Down Money Pig went and broke into many pieces!

Rag Doll: Look, I have picked up sixteen pennies, four dollar pieces, and one ten dollar piece. I have found (9) $_____.

Wagon: I have found all the rest of the pennies. I have found (10) _____ pennies.

Clock: If we are going to help Money Pig find the rest of his money, we will have to look for (11) $_____. Let's get busy!

Narrator One: Rag Doll, Wagon, and Clock searched and searched until they found (12)_____ one dollar pieces, (13)_____ five dollar pieces, and (14)_____ten dollar pieces. Then they got glue and stuck Money Pig together again and gave him back all his money.

Entire Cast: SO, with his pieces all put back together
Stuck with glue from end to end
Money Pig plays with all the toys.
For he learned that you can't buy a friend.

Answer Key: 1) 3 yards 2) 8 3) 8 4) 180 5) $92.43 6) 20 7) 1/4 8) $184.86 9) $14.16 10) 27 11) $78.27 12) 18 13) 6 14) 3

A MATH PLAY TO FIGURE OUT

KATE CRACKERNUTS

Directions: A team of six players will read through the play and work out the answers to the math problems. The team will then perform the play including the answers that are called for.

Reading Parts: Narrator One, Narrator Two, Queen, Witch, Kate, Fairy

Narrator One: A woman with a daughter married a king with a daughter. The new queen made sure that her daughter, Kate, had a bedroom 20 by 20 feet. The king's daughter, Ann, had a closet to sleep that was 3 by 3 feet. Kate had (1) _____ more square feet of space than Ann.

Queen: There must be some way to spoil Ann's beauty. I'll go ask the witch in the wood for help. It is a 6 mile walk and each mile will take me 30 minutes. It will take me (2) _____ hours to get there. But it will be worth the trip.

Witch: I see the queen approaching. She is 30 yards away, but moving 6 yards a minute. She will be here in (3) _____ minutes. She will ask me to spoil her stepdaughter's beauty. I will boil a sheep's hide and bones in my pot and tell the queen to have the girl come to me at 6:00 A.M. in the morning. It is now 6:00 P.M. in the evening. That is (4)_____ hours from now.

Narrator Two: The next morning the queen told Ann to go to the hen house and gather 6 eggs each from 36 hens, She was to take all (5) _____ eggs to the witch in the woods. Off she went with the eggs.

Witch: Here, girl, drop the eggs of 4 hens into my pot. That will be (6)_____ eggs. Now lean over and smell the brew.

Narrator One: Ann did as she was told. As she leaned over the pot, her head fell off and a sheep's head flew out of the pot and landed on her shoulders. The poor girl ran back to the castle in half the time it had taken the queen to make the one-way trip, or (7)_____ minutes.

Narrator Two: Kate, the queen's daughter, loved her half sister and was shocked to see the girl with a sheep's head instead of her own lovely face. The 2 girls left the palace and set out into the world to seek their fortunes. Kate gathered nuts to eat on the way and 42 nuts made a pound. She gathered 336 nuts or (8) _____ pounds of nuts.

Kate: Look, Ann, here is a palace I have heard about. The king has 2 sons and the youngest prince is ill and no cause can be found. The king is offering 38 gold pieces for anyone who will sit up with the prince for 3 nights. Each piece is worth $212.00. I will sit up with the prince and earn (9) $_____. A fortune!

Narrator One: Early that evening Kate hid in the prince's room. All was quiet until midnight. Then the prince rose, dressed, saddled his horse, and with Kate behind him, rode off into the night. The horse galloped at a speed of 24 miles per hour. The prince arrived in 10 minutes. He had traveled (10) _____ miles. Kate had time to snatch only a few nuts from the trees as they rode by.

Narrator Two: They reached a hill that opened wide to admit them. Inside were fairy tale ladies who led the prince away to dance. He would dance for 8 hours until dawn. Each hour he would dance with 15 different ladies or a total of (11) _____ ladies.

Kate: No wonder the prince is so tired every day. He is thin and pale because he is too tired to eat.

Narrator One: Dawn came and the prince mounted his horse with Kate behind. The prince looked paler and more ill than before. The next night, the same thing happened; but this time Kate listened to the whispering of the fairy dancers. One pointed to Kate and then to a young child holding a wand.

Fairy: See that poor girl with an apron full of nuts? She has a sister with a sheep's head. She could buy 4 ounces of bat's blood at $80 per ounce and 12 yards of spider silk at $1.49 per yard and mix them to put on her sister's head, but it would be (12) $_____ foolishly spent. If she wants her sister to have her own head again, 3 taps of that little fairy child's wand will do the trick.

Kate: I know what to do. I will roll some of these nuts across the floor and when the child runs after them I will snatch up the wand and take it with me. If it takes the child 3 minutes to gather the nuts, I can snatch the wand in 1/4 of that time or (13)_____ of a minute.

Narrator Two: That is exactly what she did. At dawn Kate and the prince rode home as before. Kate ran to Ann's room, tapped her 3 times with the wand and Ann had her own pretty head again.

Narrator One: On the third night Kate rode again with the prince to the green hill. Again she snatched nuts from the trees as they rode by. This time the child held a piece of cake. Kate overheard the fairy dancers talking.

Fairy: I hear the king and queen are most sad. The prince gets thinner and paler every day. Soon he will waste away to nothing. Too bad they don't know that 3 bites of that child's cake will cure him.

Kate: I must be faster than before to get the cake from that child. I must snatch the cake in 1/8 of the 3 minutes it will take him to gather the nuts I will spill across the floor. I must snatch the cake in (14)_____ of a minute.

Narrator Two: That is exactly what she did. At dawn Kate and the prince set off for home again. As soon as they got there, the exhausted prince lay down on his bed. Kate entered his chamber, awoke the prince and gave him 3 bites of the magic cake. He arose from his bed well and whole again.

Narrator One: Kate married the young prince and Ann married his brother and a more magnificent wedding one could not imagine. Decorations for the palace ballroom cost $2,678. Flowers for each bride cost $825.00. The feast for 2,000 guests cost $25.00 per guest. The bridal gowns trimmed in gold and diamonds were $20,000 each. The total cost of the wedding was (15) $_____.

Entire Cast: Everyone agreed it was worth every penny!

Answer Key: 1) 31 2) 3 3) 5 4) 12 5) 216 6) 24 7) 90 8) 8 9) $8,056 10) 4 11) 120 12) $337.88 13) 3/4 14) 3/8 15) $94,328.00

GOOD READING: MATHEMATICS

Amato, Mary. All published by Children's Press, 2002. (Easy Reading)
    Math at the Store
    Math in the Backyard
    Math in the Car
    Math in the Kitchen
    Math in the Neighborhood
    Math on the Playground

Chrismer, Melanie. *Multiply This!* Children's Press, 2005.

Clemson, Wendy. All published by Gareth Stevens, 2005.
    Using Math to Be a Zoo Vet
    Using Math to Conquer Extreme Sports
    Using Math to Solve a Crime

Clements, Andrew. *A Million Dots.* Simon & Schuster, 2006.

Lewis, J. Patrick. *Arithme-Tickle: An Even Number of Odd Riddle Rhymes.* Harcourt, 2007.

Neuschwander, Cindy
    Mummy Math. Holt, 2005.
    Sir Cumference and the Dragon. Charlesbridge, 1999.
    Sir Cumference and the First Round Table. Charlesbridge, 1997.
    Sir Cumference and the Great Knight of Angleland. Charlesbridge, 2001.
    Sir Cumference and the Sword in the Cone. Charlesbridge, 2003.

Sargent, Brian. All published by Children's Press, 2005.
    Can You Guess?
    Everyone Uses Math
    How Heavy Is It?

Schwartz, David
    How Much Is a Million? Lothrop, 1985.
    On Beyond a Million. Doubleday, 1999.

Tang, Greg. All published by Scholastic.
    The Grapes of Math. 2004.
    Math Appeal. 2003.
    Math Fables. 2004.
    Math Potatoes: Mind-Stretching Brain Food. 2005.
    Math-Terpieces. 2003.

Part Three

Geography

The Earth is a heavy burden because . . .

EXPLORERS

Number of Players: Teams of three.

Objective: To recall and orally report information on several explorers.

Procedure: One player takes the part of the interviewer. A second player takes the part of an explorer. The explorer answers questions about his voyage(s) that are asked by the interviewer. Another player kneels behind the explorer and acts out appropriate hand gestures.

Follow Up: Introduce books on explorers and exploration.

Possible Interviews

Amerigo Vespucci (1454-1512)
  Tells of his discovery of mainland America in 1497.

Christopher Columbus (1451-1506)
  Tells of one or more of four voyages to the new world, returning to Spain with strange plants, spices, and gold.

Juan Ponce deLeon (1460-1521)
  Tells of his discovery of Florida while seeking the Fountain of Youth.

Hernando De Soto (1500-1542)
  Tells of his discovery of the Mississippi River and describes the river and surrounding vegetation.

Sir Francis Drake (1540-1596)
  Tells how his ship became the first to sail around the world and why the Spanish called him "El Draque," or the dragon.

Ferdinand Magellan (1480-1521)
  Tells of his voyage sailing around the tip of South America and discovering the Pacific Ocean.

Henry Hudson (1565-1611?)
  Tells of the four dangerous voyages he made in search of a Northeast Passage and how he and his crew survived the cold Arctic winters.

Good Reading: *Explorer* by Rupert Matthews. DK Publishers, 2000.

A GIFT FOR THE QUEEN

Number of Players: Five

Objective: To identify items native to a particular environment.

Procedure: Four players take the parts of explorers. Player one has just returned from a desert. Player two has returned from the Arctic. Player three has returned from a tropical island. Player four has returned from the coast and forests of North America.

The explorers approach the Queen one at a time. Each offers a gift brought from the area of exploration. Each wants to please the Queen and be allowed to sit in a special chair at her side. Each will extol the value of the gift he/she has brought. The gift must be something found only in the habitat the explorer has visited. The way the gift is described and presented is more important than the gift itself. After each explorer has presented his/her gift, the Queen can make her choice or the audience can vote on the best presentation and the winner takes his/her place at the Queen's side.

Possible Gifts

Desert	Arctic
Rattlesnake	Blubber
Vulture	Walrus Tusk
Cactus	Polar Bear Cub
Cactus Flower	Block of Ice
Box of Sand	

Tropical Island	Forest
Coconut	Small Pine Tree
Palm Tree	Baby Rabbit
Piece of Lava	Wildflowers
Pineapple	Turtle Shell

Good Reading: *Planet Earth Inside Out* by Gail Gibbons. Morrow Jr. Books, 1995.

GEOGRAPHY TERMS

Play the X Game!

Number of Players: Varies

Objective: To introduce geographic terms.

Directions: Select a geography term to write on the chalkboard. However, rather than letters, use Xs for the correct number of letters in the word.

Example: X X X X X tells those who are guessing that there are five letters in this word. Students take turns guessing a letter. For example: a student might guess (correctly) that the third letter is L. This X is then erased and the letter L put in its place. If the student cannot then guess the word, another student takes a turn in guessing another letter. A student can only guess the geographic term if a letter is guessed correctly.

Follow Up: Share a variety of world atlases.

continent	mountain	isthmus	desert
summit	latitude	lowland	swamp
continent	plain	pinnacle	bayou
hemisphere	arroyo	glacier	Antarctic
island	isthmus	estuary	delta
peninsula	oasis	savannah	plateau
precipice	longitude	valley	wetland

May be copied for classroom use. *From Get Up and Move with Nonfiction* by Nancy Polette.
Westport, CT: Teacher Ideas Press. Copyright © 2008.

CATEGORIES

Number of Players: One for each category used.

Objective: To name many items within a given category.

Procedure: Mark off from one end of a room to the other with chalk marks 18 inches apart. Players begin at one end of the room. A leader gives a player a category [*example*: Countries of Central and South America]. For each country the player can name within 30 seconds, the player takes one step forward. When the player can no longer name items in the category, or time expires, the steps are counted to see how far the player has come.

A second player is given a different category and moves in the same way. The winner is the player who moves the greatest distance.

Follow Up: Share a variety of world atlases.

Countries of Central and South America
Countries of Europe
States of the United States
Provinces of Canada

"On Your Feet" Activity

Two players find out more about one of the countries, states, or provinces named and summarize the information, taking turns, one line at a time in a acrostic poem.

Example:

- M iddle of the United States
- I ndustries include aircraft manufacture
- S how Me State
- S t. Louis is a major city
- O zark Mountains
- U nder France from 1673 until 1764
- R ivers include the Missouri and Mississippi
- I nteresting citizens: Mark Twain, Molly Brown, Harry Truman

PLACES IN THE WORLD

Number of Players: Any number can play.

Objective: To share prior knowledge about cities, states, provinces, and countries of the world.

Procedure: Players sit in a circle. One player names a city, state, province, or country. The player on the left names a different city, state, province, or country—but the name must begin with the LAST letter of the previous word.

Follow Up: Share a variety of world atlases.

Example:

DETROIT   TRENTON   NEW JERSEY   YUKON   NORTH DAKOTA

Variations: Limit the names to . . .

- Countries of the World
- Cities of the World
- Cities and States of the United States
- Cities and Provinces of Canada
- Cities and Countries of Europe
- Cities and Countries of Asia
- Cities and Countries of Africa
- Cities and Countries of Central and South America
- Cities and States of Australia

Good Reading: *Rand McNally Atlas of the World.* Metro Books, 2003; *The Ultimate Interactive Atlas of the World.* Scholastic, 2007

ALPHABET TRAVELS

Number of players: Any number can play.

Objective: To use alliteration in sharing prior knowledge about countries of the world.

Procedure: Players form a circle. The object of the game is to go through the entire alphabet using as many words as possible that begin with a particular letter. It is helpful to give each person the name of a country beforehand to give players time to think. The letter X can be eliminated.

Examples:

I am going to Australia to see agreeable alligators.

I am going to Brazil to bring back bundles of bananas.

I am going to Jordan to juggle jelly beans.

I am going to Denmark to devour delicious dinners.

ABC Names: Other names can be substituted.

Afghanistan	Netherlands
Bosnia	Okinawa
Canada	Portugal
Denmark	Qatar
Egypt	Russia
France	Sweden
Greece	Turkey
Haiti	Uruguay
India	Vietnam
Jordan	Wales
Korea	Yugoslavia
Labrador	Zambia
Malta	

Good Reading: *Rand McNally Atlas of the World.* Metro Books, 2003; *The Ultimate Interactive Atlas of the World.* Scholastic, 2007

INTRODUCTIONS

Number of Players: Any number can play.

Objective: To associate an animal and product that begin with the same letter as the country where they are found.

Procedure: Each player names a country that begins with the same first letter of his or her first name. The player will then name one product and one animal whose names begin with the same letter as the player's first name.
Players introduce themselves in turn, using this pattern.

My name is **Gladys**

My best friend's name is **George**

We come from **Great Britain**

We sell **glassware**

We both like **goats**

Expand the Pattern

Through research, find more items produced and native animals that begin with the same letter as the country, province, or state.

Example

My name is Gladys

My best friend's name is Gregory

We come from Great Britain

We sell glassware, grapes, gravel, gloves, government tours

We both like grasshoppers and guinea pigs

Good Reading: *Rand McNally Atlas of the World.* Metro Books, 2003. *The Ultimate Interactive Atlas of the World.* Scholastic, 2007

MY AUNT CAME BACK

Number of Players: Any number can play.

Objective: To name places in the world and include the name in a rhyme.

Procedure: Players can sit in a circle or in rows. Each player will say a rhyme that contains the name of a city, state, province, or country.

Examples:

My aunt came back
From old Brazil
And brought to me
A sleeping pill.

My aunt came back
From Afghanistan
And brought to me
A frying pan

My aunt came back
From Holland, too
And brought to me
A wooden shoe

My aunt came back
From London town
And brought to me
A brand new gown

My aunt came back
From old Japan
And brought to me
A pretty fan

[*All say the last verse*]
My aunt came back
From Timbuktu
And brought to me
Some nuts like you!

Good Reading: *Rand McNally Atlas of the World.* Metro Books, 2003; *The Ultimate Interactive Atlas of the World.* Scholastic, 2007

CIRCLE GAMES

Number of Players: Teams numbering six to ten players each.

Objective: To draw on prior knowledge of geographic terms or places in the world (cities, countries, states, provinces).

Procedure: Each team chooses a person on the team to be the starter. Teams must have the same number of players. A judge is appointed to listen to the responses of each team and to rule if a response is repeated or if a response is incorrect. The player giving a repeated or incorrect response must give a correct response before the circle responses can continue. The circle that finishes first is the winner.

Topics: (For six player circles)

Name 24 of the 50 states in the United States.

Name 24 different capitals of the 50 states.

Name the Provinces of Canada

Name 12 of the countries in North and South America

Name 12 different rivers of the World.

Name 12 different countries in Europe.

Name 6 different countries in Asia.

Name 6 deserts of the World.

Name 6 oceans of the World.

Good Reading: *Celebrating the Fifty States* by Loreen Leedy. Holiday House, 1999; *National Geographic Atlas of the World.* National Geographic, 2007.

MEET A LANDFORM

Number of Players: Number can vary.

Objective: To understand and use personification. To become acquainted with definitions for a variety of landforms.

Procedure: Each player must find a definition of a landform and begin by introducing himself or herself as one of the landforms listed below. The player then states two things he or she (as the landform) can do that a person can do. Players can be as creative as they wish in their introductions.

continent	island	mountain	isthmus	plateau
plain	desert	swamp	valley	peninsula
a pinnacle	summit	bog	glacier	oasis
bayou	lowland	ravine	marsh	savannah
mirage	dunes	mesa	butte	arroyo

Examples:

You can't keep me from showing off! My name is Mountain and I **stretch up** to **cut** through the clouds and **stand strong** as the tallest giant against the wind that cannot blow me away.

I am a **collector** of countries. My body **spreads** out over a large area. I rarely **grow** any larger but sometimes the oceans eat away at my sides. I am a continent.

Lots of vegetation covers my dark **body.** I **creep** around twisted trees and tall weeds. **My children** are alligators and snakes. Most people avoid me. I am a swamp.

Good Reading: *Hottest, Coldest, Highest, Deepest* by Steve Jenkins. Houghton-Mifflin, 1998.

MEET A WEATHER PHENOMENON

Number of Players: Number can vary.

Objective: To understand and use similes to become acquainted with definitions for a variety of weather phenomenons.

Procedure: Each player must find a definition of a weather phenomenon and begin by introducing himself or herself as one of the terms listed below. The player then states two things he or she (as the phenomenon) is like. Players can be as creative as they wish in their introductions.

ice	snow	tornado	hurricane
monsoon	tsunami	rain	thunderstorm
blizzard	chinook	cloudburst	dew
drought	fog	frost	hail
jet stream	mistral	lightning	rainbow
sleet	norther	thunder	typhoon

Example:

Round and round I go! My name is Tornado and my dusty funnel is like an elephant's trunk sucking up the world's debris like a giant vacuum cleaner.

Create A Chant

Two players learn more about one of the weather terms listed above. Two words at a time, in turn, each player describes the term until each has given six two-word descriptions

Example:

A FOG CHANT

Player One	*Player Two*
Clear nights,	Gentle winds
Chill layers	Warm air
Above the earth,	Mixing it
With cold air,	At the surface
Fog forms,	Drains down
Lowest point,	Of the ground

Good Reading: *Science Book of Weather* by Neil Ardley. Guliver, 2002; *The Storm* compiled by Barbara McGrath. Charlesbridge, 2006.

THE TIC TAC GEOGRAPHY EXCUSE

Number of Players: One

Objective: The student will associate unlike items to develop a monologue.

Procedure: The player will choose any three items in a row and use the three items in an excuse as to why something was not done.

Social Studies
Why did you get lost in the desert?

hemisphere	estuary	delta
boundary	latitude	jet stream
arroyo	continent	foliage

Geography
Why did your expedition fail to arrive at the top of Mount Everest?

Antarctic	blizzard	earthquake
eclipse	compass	fossil
glacier	precipice	resources

Good Reading: *The Top of the World: Climbing Mount Everest* by Steve Jenkins. Houghton-Mifflin, 1999.

A PREPOSITION PRAIRIE

Number of Players: Four to six.

Objective: To demonstrate comprehension of nonfiction text about prairies by creating and sharing orally a preposition poem.

Procedure: The team chooses a prairie animal. [*Example*: prairie chicken.] Each team member chooses a preposition: over, under, on, between, etc. In reading about the prairie, team members will note all the places or things the animal could be over, under, between, etc. Team members then line up to share the lines in their preposition poem.

Choose one of the prairie animals mentioned in the text you read. Use the pattern below to create a four to six line preposition poem about the animal. Use factual information in your poem.

Example:

In the tall tall grass

By the shallow river valleys

Under a haystack

Between low hills

Lives a prairie chicken named Perky.

Your Turn:

In the _____

By the _____

Under _____

Over _____

Around _____

Between _____

Lives a _____ named _____.

Good Reading: *My Face in the Wind: A Prairie Teacher* by Jim Murphy Scholastic, 2001.

May be copied for classroom use. *From Get Up and Move with Nonfiction* by Nancy Polette. Westport, CT: Teacher Ideas Press. Copyright © 2008.

SINGING ABOUT RIVERS

Number of Players: Number can vary.

Objective: To demonstrate comprehension of text about one or more rivers by encoding the information in a song.

Procedure: The team will read and list facts about one or more rivers. The facts will be included in a song that the team will sing for the class.

Example:

The Mighty Mississippi is fed by tributary rivers from 33 states and two Canadian provinces. It begins as a tiny brook and 2,350 miles later empties into the Gulf of Mexico. It has always been a working river. An average of 175 million tons of freight is shipped each year on the Upper Mississippi. The 29 lock and dams on the Upper Mississippi make that shipping possible, allowing for navigation from St. Louis, Missouri, to Saint Paul, Minnesota, a total distance of 854 miles. There are records of human habitation along the Mississippi River that date back more than 5,000 years. The Mississippi River basin was formed by glaciers, moving and melting millions of years ago, which left in their wake sometimes miles-wide floodplains that still fill up occasionally, covering towns, roads, farms, and everything else that might stand in the way of its mighty waters.

Sing A Song About the Mississippi

Sing to the tune of "Yellow Rose of Texas."

Oh the (1) M_____ River
You must come and take a look
The longest in the nation
Began as a small (2) b_____

A two thousand plus mile river
Big black barges piled with (3) f_____
They move like bugs in water
Making sure they won't be late.

Good Reading: *Mississippi River* by Peter Lourie. Boyds Mill, 2001; *Rio Grande* by Peter Lourie. Boyds Mill, 2001.

Answer Key: 1. Mississippi 2. brook 3. freight

RIVERS, OCEANS, AND SEAS

Number of Players: Any number can play.

Objective: To review knowledge about a particular river or ocean.

Procedure: Names of rivers, oceans, and seas are written on separate cards. Each player takes a card and moves around randomly until one player begins to speak. All other players freeze while the speaker talks about the river or ocean listed on his/her card. The speaker can indicate the next speaker by looking or gesturing to them. When that player begins to talk, the first speaker freezes. The game continues until all players holding cards have spoken.

MAJOR RIVERS	MAJOR OCEANS
Allegheny	Pacific Ocean
Amazon	Atlantic Ocean
Arkansas	Indian Ocean
Colorado	Arctic Ocean
Columbia	South China Sea
Delaware	Mediterranean Sea
Hudson	Bering Sea
Illinois	Sea of Japan
Mississippi	East China Sea
Missouri	Black Sea
Nile	Red Sea
Ohio	North Sea
Platte	Baltic Sea
Potomac	Yellow Sea
Rio Grande	
St. Lawrence	
Wabash	
Yukon	

Variation
This game can be used with any geographic areas (cities, countries, states, provinces)

Good Reading: *The Vast Mysterious Deep* by David Harrison. Boyds Mill, 2004; *Rivers: Nature's Wondrous Waterways* by David Harrison. Boyds Mill, 2002.

A RHYMING ARCTIC ADVENTURE

Number of Players: Any number can play.

Objective: To demonstrate comprehension of Arctic terms.

Procedure: Each player gives two lines that demonstrate understanding of one of the terms below. The last words in the lines must rhyme.

Antarctica	permafrost	Arctic Circle	glacier	petroleum
mosses	lichens	tundra	calving	reindeer
caribou	lemmings	voles	foxes	seals

Examples:

    Antarctica is 8,000 feet high
    What an elevation, my, oh my!

    Arctic foxes like the snow
    Dig a cave and in they go

    Believe me, it is true
    Glaciers are not white but blue

Good Reading: *Into the Ice Age: The Story of Arctic Exploration* by Lynn Curlee. Houghton-Mifflin, 1998.

CREATE AN ENVIRONMENT

Number of Players: Teams of six.

Objective: To re-create an identifiable environment using mime.

Directions: Each team receives an environment card. Team members have 5 minutes to discuss the landforms, vegetation, animals, weather, etc., typical of the environment and to assign parts. [*Example*: In the Rain Forest, players might take the parts of trees, rain, a jaguar, a snake, etc.]

No words are spoken; although sound effects can be used (the pitter patter of the rain, the roar of the jaguar, etc.). When the audience guesses the environment, another team takes the stage to demonstrate their environment.

Follow Up: Share books about protecting the environment.

Environment Cards

Rain Forest	Tropical Island	Arctic
Desert	Mountain	River Bank
Forest	Great Plains	Swamp

Good Reading: *Environmental Disaster Alert* by Paul Challen. Crabtree, 2005

THE FIFTY STATES

Number of Players: Eight teams of two to four players.

Objective: To be able to place states within the various regions of the United States.

Directions: Teams are given the names of states within various regions of the United States. Each team will make a sentence using the first letter of each state, then create a story that ends with the sentence.

Follow Up: Share books about the fifty states.

Example:

ROCKY MOUNTAIN STATES

C-COLORADO I-IDAHO N-NEVADA W-WYOMING M-MONTANA U-UTAH

Cool Ike Never Wore Mended Underwear.

Cool Ike was just about the best guide the Rocky Mountains had ever known. Folks came from all over the world to be led by Ike across Colorado's Continental Divide, explore a Crystal Ice Cave in Idaho, or go birdwatching for the Mountain Bluebirds of Nevada. Nobody could remember a time when Cool Ike hadn't been around. Folks in Wyoming swore that Cool Ike was older than Old Faithful. Year after year he led folks through the Big Sky country of Montana and across Utah's Rainbow Bridge. Cool Ike was so popular that his hiking tours were booked up months in advance. He liked to brag that he had never lost a hiker.

A trip with Cool Ike was something to remember. Hikers would trail behind the spritely old man, wiping sweat from their brows as they climbed higher and higher. One thing folks noticed about Cool Ike was, that no matter how high or how far he climbed, he never wiped a single bead of sweat from his brow. Even more surprising, when the hikers stopped to drink from their canteens, Cool Ike never took a sip of water. "Amazing!" they all said. "It's hotter than spit on a griddle. How can that old man move so fast and climb so high without breaking a sweat and needing a drink of water?"

Ike never told anyone his secret. Being a mountain man, he never got to the city. So when his underwear got holes, he didn't bother to sew them up. The mountain breezes could just flow right through. That was how Ike kept cool because **Cool Ike never wore mended underwear.**

Good Reading: *Celebrating the Fifty States* by Loreen Leedy. Holiday House, 1999.

MNEMONICS CHALLENGE

THE FIFTY STATES

Directions: Each team receives one of the following strips. The team will create a sentence using the first letter of each state and a story that ends with that sentence.

MID ATLANTIC STATES	
N-NEW YORK	N-NEW JERSEY
M-MARYLAND	P-PENNSYLVANIA
D-DELAWARE	D-D.C.

NEW ENGLAND STATES	
C-CONNECTICUT	R-RHODE ISLAND
M-MAINE	M-MASSACHUSETTS
N-NEW HAMPSHIRE	V-VERMONT

SOUTH ATLANTIC STATES	
V-VIRGINIA	S-SOUTH CAROLINA
W-WEST VIRGINIA	F-FLORIDA
N-NORTH CAROLINA	G-GEORGIA

SOUTHERN STATES	
A-ALABAMA	T-TENNESSEE
A-ARKANSAS	M-MISSISSIPPI
K-KENTUCKY	L-LOUISIANA

UPPER MIDWESTERN STATES	
S-SOUTH DAKOTA	M-MINNESOTA
N-NORTH DAKOTA	W-WISCONSIN
M-MICHIGAN	

LOWER MIDWESTERN STATES	
M-MISSOURI	I-IOWA
I-ILLINOIS	K-KANSAS
I-INDIANA	O-OHIO
N-NEBRASKA	

SOUTHWESTERN STATES	
O-OKLAHOMA	T-TEXAS
A-ARIZONA	N-NEW MEXICO

PACIFIC COAST STATES	
A-ALASKA	O-OREGON
H-HAWAII	W-WASHINGTON
C-CALIFORNIA	

THE MYSTERY GAME

Number of Players: One, plus the audience.

Objective: To report on any city in the world by encoding information in a new format.

Procedure: The player researches and writes ten clues (facts) about a city. List the ten clues in random order. One fact must be a "give away" clue, one that will easily identify the city.

Follow Up: Share books about cities that have faced and overcome disasters.

Example:

1. I once had many shoe factories.
2. The Forest Park Zoo is a major attraction.
3. Flower lovers enjoy Shaw's Garden.
4. Actress, Betty Grable, was born here.
5. The city has an outdoor Municipal Opera.
6. Most people recognize the Gateway Arch.
7. This large city was never the State Capital.
8. The city has a large Italian population.
9. Art Hill is a popular place to sledders.
10. The city was founded by the French.

Play the Game

One student in the group says a number between one and ten. The clue for that number is read. The student can guess or pass. If the student passes or does not guess correctly, then another student can give a number. The game continues until the country, state, or province is guessed or all of the numbers are used.

Good Reading: *City of Snow: The Great Blizzard of 1888* by Linda High. Walker, 2004; *City Not Forsaken* by Lynn & Gilbert Morris. Bethel Publishers, 1995.

COMPARING COUNTRIES

Number of Players: Two teams of two to four players and a leader.

Objective: To become familiar with the land and cultures of several countries.

Procedure: Players are responsible for researching basic facts about the land and culture of several countries. Write each country's name on a separate index card or slip of paper. A leader chooses two cards. Members of Team One must name all the ways the two countries are alike within a one minute period. At the end of time, the leader chooses two more cards. Members of Team Two must name all the ways the two countries are alike within a one minute period.

After three rounds, the team with the most correct responses wins.

Note: At the end of a one minute period a member of the opposite team can challenge a response, which must be justified. The leader makes the final decision as to whether a response can count. (The leader should have available information cards on each country.)

Good Reading: *Around the World in A Hundred Years* by Jean Fritz. Putnam, 1994.

GIANT SENTENCES

THE CARIBBEAN

Number of Players: Two to four teams of six.

Objective: To show understanding of words related to the Caribbean by using them in a giant sentence.

Procedure: Each player on a team is given two words from the word list. The first team member starts a sentence that includes his/her two words. Team members, in turn, continue the sentence being sure to include their two words. Words must be used correctly. Each team is timed. The team that uses all of its words correctly in completing the giant sentence is the winner.

Follow Up: Share books about the Caribbean islands.

Team One	Team Two	Team Three	Team Four
Caribbean	West Indies	suntan	sand
tropical	calypso	conch	beaches
Cuba	conga	coral	patois
hurricane	palms	diving	English
tourists	fishing	mangos	reggae
snorkeling	bananas	Columbus	limbo
cruise	boats	warm	swim
80volcanoes	Trinidad	French	shells
steel drums	markets	reefs	island
Jamaica	Tobago	Antigua	Guadeloupe

Good Reading: *Caribbean Counting Book* by Charles Faustin. Houghton Mifflin, 1996.

CANADIAN WHERE AM I?

Number of Players: Any number can play.

Objective: To share information about the provinces of Canada.

Procedure: Players sit in a circle. Each player picks a card from a container. On the card is the name of a Canadian province or territory. In the center of the circle are stuffed toys. The student chosen to go first selects one of the stuffed toys and talks to it as if it were alive, describing the province or territory listed on the card. The first player in the circle who guesses the location is the next player.

Follow Up: Share books about the Canadian provinces and territories.

Canadian Provinces and Territories

Alberta	British Columbia	Manitoba
New Brunswick	Newfoundland	Nova Scotia
Ontario	Quebec	Prince Edward Island
Saskatchewan	Northwest Territories	Yukon Territory
Nunavut		

Good Reading: *Canada from A to Z* by Bobbie Kalman. Children's Press, 2005.

TOURIST ATTRACTION

Number of Players: Teams of four.

Objective: To creatively relate information about a country.

Procedure: Each team researches a major city of the world. The team creates a radio commercial to lure tourists to visit the city. The commercial must contain a chant or song, which will be performed.

Example:

Chant	Song: (Tune: "London Bridge")
Facts about London	London town is the place to see
Queen's Palace	The palace where
Big Ben	The Queen will be
Royal Guard	See the changing of the guard
Piccadilly Square	Let's go visit.
Tower of London	
Royal jewels	London Town is the place to go
Dress of midnight blue	Tower of London
Downing Street	Quite a show
Scotland Yard	Hear Big Ben give out the time
British Museum	Let's go visit
Jack the Ripper	
London Bridge	Downing Street and Piccadilly Square
Theatre Row	London Bridge
Queen's corgis, too	Is standing there.
Let's all go	Scotland Yard and the
Now you know	British Museum
Facts about London	Let's go visit.

Good Reading: *World Almanac for Kids, 2007.* World Almanac Books, 2007.

STORYTELLING IN GEOGRAPHY

THE JOURNEY CIRCLE STORY

Number of Players: Four

Objective: Four players will tell a circle story that describes four different places.

Procedure: The teacher or leader tells a circle story. [*Example*: In *Alamo Across Texas* by Jill Stover, Alamo the alligator has to find a new home. Each place he tries has something wrong with it so he moves to the next new home and finally ends up back in his original home on the river.]

Each student chooses a place and discovers its location, three sights, at least one meaningful fact, and why a person would want to leave this place. Information is recorded on a circle chart.

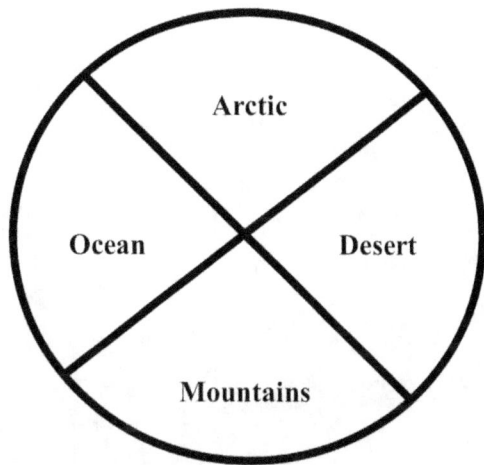

Sample Story:

Once there was an albatross who liked his Arctic home where he was never bothered by tourists. The polar bears that wandered about the frozen peaks were his friends. He had good fish to eat, and there was no housing shortage. He could nest wherever he wished. But the albatross disliked one thing about the Arctic. In the winter time there was no daylight for six months. So one day he left the Arctic and went looking for sunshine.

The albatross found plenty of sunshine in the hot, dry desert. He made friends with the prairie dogs and lizards. He watched the cactus bloom in the spring. But the albatross did not like gila monsters. After his third encounter with one, he left the desert and flew to the mountains.

(Continued)

The albatross loved the cool breezes in the mountains. He flew from one majestic peak to another. He made friends with the mountain goats and with the mountain gorillas in Africa. But he didn't care much for their diet of bugs and juicy termites. The albatross missed having fish for breakfast so he left the mountains and flew over the ocean.

He dove into the water and caught just the right fish for his breakfast. The salt water sprayed up on his wings. Ships passed in the night. Finally the albatross got tired of tourists on cruise ships pointing and calling out to him. He left the ocean and flew back to the Arctic where he lives today eating fish whenever he wishes and enjoying his privacy.

STRANGE DESTINATIONS

Use the descriptions on the next two pages to complete the information asked for below and tell the story. Information can be written in each section of the circle. Create a character to make the journey from one place to the next. Be sure to tell why the character would want to leave.

Lost Civilizations and Mysterious Places

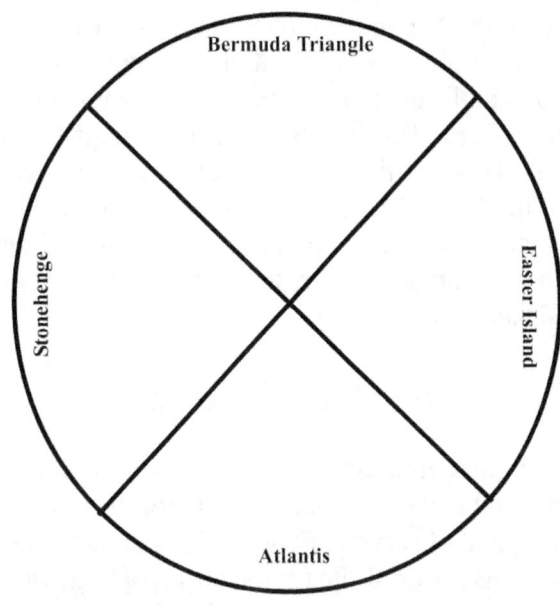

I am _____.

Those who visit me see (*list at least three sights*) _____
_____.

I am controversial because (*one strong reason*) _____
_____.

The most meaningful fact about me is _____.

One reason people leave me is _____.

Good Reading: *Strange Mysteries from Around the World* by Seymour Simon. William Morrow, 1997

DESTINATIONS

BERMUDA TRIANGLE

The Bermuda Triangle is an imaginary triangle stretching from the warm seas of Florida to beautiful Bermuda and Puerto Rico. Stories of the Triangle have been told of curses, methane gas, sea monsters, and deadly tides. In 1492, Columbus's compass went haywire and he and his crew saw a "great flame of fire" that crashed into the ocean. In 1872 the *Mary Celeste* was found abandoned in the triangle with no sign of the crew. On December 5, 1945, with the famed disappearance of Flight 19, five Navy Avenger bombers mysteriously vanished while on a routine training mission, as did a rescue plane sent to search for them—six aircraft and 27 men, gone without a trace. A few hazards in the area of the Bermuda Triangle do contribute to the accidents that occur in the wide swath of sea. The first is the lack of magnetic declination near 80° west (just off the coast of Miami). This agonic line is one of two points on the earth's surface where compasses point directly to the North Pole, versus to the Magnetic North Pole elsewhere on the planet. The change in declination can make compass navigation difficult. Despite its reputation, visitors often travel through the triangle to enjoy the warm breezes, beautiful beaches, and casual lifestyles found on Bermuda and Puerto Rico.

STONEHENGE

Stonehenge is surely Britain's greatest national icon, symbolizing mystery, power, and endurance. Some have speculated that it was a temple made for the worship of ancient earth deities. It has been called an astronomical observatory for marking significant events on the prehistoric calendar. Others claim that it was a sacred site for the burial of high-ranking citizens from the societies of long ago. Stonehenge was a large earthwork; a bank and ditch arrangement called a henge, constructed approximately 5,000 years ago. It is believed that the ditch was dug with tools made from the antlers of red deer and, possibly, wood. The legend of King Arthur provides a story of the construction of Stonehenge. It seems that Merlin brought the stones to the Salisbury Plain from Ireland where they were used for performing rituals and for healing. Led by King Uther and Merlin, the expedition arrived at the spot in Ireland. The Britons, none of whom were giants, apparently, were unsuccessful in their attempts to move the great stones. At this point, Merlin realized that only his magic arts would do the trick. So, they were dismantled and shipped back to Britain where they were set up. Despite all its dilapidation and the encroachment of the modern world, Stonehenge, today, is an awe-inspiring sight.

DESTINATIONS

EASTER ISLAND

One of the most mystifying places on Earth, located 2,300 miles off the west coast of Chile, Easter Island is the world's most isolated inhabited island where the people developed their own distinctive culture best known by the moai, huge figures carved of volcanic rock. Hundreds of these sculpted monoliths dot the landscape, some in imposing rows, others toppled, broken, and scarred by violence. All of the residents of Easter Island live in the town of Hanga Roa, and it is an easy day's drive from town around the island in search of the rectangular stone platforms where moai were mounted. One of the most famous sites on the island is Rano Raraku, where 70 moai seem to rise from the earth. The restored village of Orongo offers another Easter Island mystery. The village sits in a spectacular setting, between the volcano of Rano Kao and a sheer cliff drop-off. Rocks found at the village contain 150 carvings showing figures with a man's body and a bird's head. Anthropologists believe they were part of a religious cult, but the details on the "Bird Man" are still obscure. To add to its mystery, today Easter Island is moving eastward toward South America by sea floor spreading at the fastest rate known in the world.

THE LOST CITY OF ATLANTIS

The story of Atlantis is found in the writings of Plato. At the very beginning of time the immortal gods divided the world among themselves. The god Poseidon received Atlantis, a vast island-continent, west of the Mediterranean, surrounded by the Atlantic Ocean. The residents were peaceful, wealthy, and advanced for the time period. The island was a capital of trade and abundant with natural resources, with a climate so perfect, each year produced not one, but two harvests. But the civilization vanished in just one day and one night. Greed and corruption had entered their world, so the Gods punished the residents, or so the legend goes. Some type of massive geological event sucked Atlantis into the sea, leaving many to believe either an earthquake or volcanic eruption was to blame. The possible location of Atlantis is Santorini in Greece. Experts believe a large section of the bay on Santorini's western shore once contained a volcano. When the eruption happened (around 17th century BC) a large portion of the island collapsed and formed a caldera. Many have asserted Plato must have believed in the island's existence because he included so much telling detail in it description.

WHAT COLOR IS IT?

Niagara Falls

Number of Players: Four to six.

Objective: To give a clear description of a setting by adding color words.

Procedure: Each player in turn will read a sentence strip adding as many color words as possible. Sentences are from a description of Niagara Falls by Mark Twain.

1. We now began to creep along bridges of a single plank, making our way by a wooden railing.
2. The sprays from the Falls rained down on us in sheets.
3. Ferns and vegetation slapped our faces.
4. Wind rushed out from behind the waterfall.
5. The wind seemed determined to sweep us from the bridge, and scatter us on the rocks and among the torrents below.
6. I looked up at the clouds in the sky.
7. Then we were almost under the wall of water thundering down from above.
8. Boulders were overwhelmed by the vegetation surrounding them.

One Minute Description

In one minute, describe a familiar place. Use as many color words as you can.

SPEAKING GERMAN

Number of Players: Two

Objective: To discover the similarities between the German and English languages.

Procedure: Two players will begin a conversation about a proposed trip to Germany. Each has been studying the German language and wants to try it out on the other before making the trip. Language strips are cut apart and laid face down. In the course of the conversation each player, in turn, picks up a strip and uses it in the conversation. The game ends when all strips have been used.

Mutter ist zu hause. (Mother is at home.)
10 x 10 ist ein hundert (10 x 10 is a hundred.)
Wo ist vater? (Where is father?)
Der mann telephoniert. (The man telephones.)
Freitag ist der beste tag. (Friday is the best day.)
Die katze miaut. (The cat meows.)
Mein auto ist nicht neu. (My car is not new.)
Der hund bellt laut. (The dog barks loudly.)
Mein haus ist in Muhlenberg. (My house is in Muhlenberg.)
Mein onkel singt sehr gut. (My uncle sings very well.)

SPEAKING STRINE

Number of Players: Two

Objective: The British who settled in Australia had to develop a vocabulary to describe the many unfamiliar animals and plants in their new home. They also brought with them some British words and phrases. This language is called "Strine." Players will become familiar with a variety of new words in this language.

Procedure: Two players will begin a conversation about a proposed trip to Australia. Each has been studying Strine and wants to try it out on the other before making the trip. Words are cut apart and laid face down. In the course of the conversation each player, in turn, picks up two words and uses it in the conversation. The game ends when each player has used eight words. See more words and their definitions on the following page.

g'day hello	bonzer great	bloke man	nipper child
cobber friend	mate best friend	jackaroo boy rancher	jillaroo girl rancher
dinki-di real thing	dinkum honest	billy kettle	barby barbecue
tucker food	rissoles burgers	snags hot dogs	tom sauce catsup
damper bread	lollies candy	icypoles popsicles	biscuits crackers

cozzie	petrol	swag	ute
swim suit	gasoline	belongings	pickup truck
bush	grazier	billabong	squatter
outback	ranch	water hole	ranch owner
nick off	ta	okie dokie	walkabout
get lost	thanks	okay	to wander
bushranger	walloper	jumbuck	chook
outlaw	policeman	sheep	chicken
roo	mossies	Mum	beaut
kangaroo	mosquitoes	mother	great
dunny	Oz	lolly water	onkey-dorey
toilet	Australia	soft drink	good

PLAY WORLD TRAVELER

Number of Players: Any number can play.

Objective: To associate great cities of the world with a major event, person or important object.

Procedure: Distribute World Bingo sheets (page 105). Cut apart the strips below and place in a container. The caller selects strips one at a time and reads the strip. The bingo player puts an X on the country that fits the object, event, or person on the strip. When all spaces in a row have Xs, the player shouts: WORLD TRAVELER!

Hear Big Ben strike [London]
See the Mona Lisa at the Louvre [Paris]
Ride a gondola on the Grand Canal [Venice]
Visit the Little Mermaid statue in the harbor [Copenhagen]
Enjoy the Octoberfest [Munich]
Attend a Chopin concert [Warsaw]
Visit St. Basil's Church on Red Square [Moscow]
Ride a camel to the Pyramids [Giza]
Go on a safari [Kenya]
Visit a mosque [Istanbul]
Explore the caves on Elephanti Island [Bombay]
Walk along the Great Wall [Peking]
Ride the Bullet Train [Tokyo]
Visit the WWII Memorial, the *Arizona* [Honolulu]
Ride a tram to the top of the Arch [St. Louis]
Visit the site of the Klondike Gold Rush [Yukon]
Ride a boat on the Amazon River [Brazil]
Shop underground [Toronto]
Visit the Parthenon [Greece]
Snorkel in the Great Barrier Reef [Queensland]
Visit active volcanoes [Hawaii]
Stroll through St. Peter's Square [Rome]
Visit the Alamo [Texas]

May be copied for classroom use. *From Get Up and Move with Nonfiction* by Nancy Polette. Westport, CT: Teacher Ideas Press. Copyright © 2008.

World Bingo

London	Paris	Venice	Munich	Copenhagen
Warsaw	Moscow	Giza	Kenya	Istanbul
Bombay	Peking	Tokyo	Honolulu	St. Louis
Yukon	Brazil	Toronto	Athens	Queensland
Hawaii	Rome	Texas	Yucatan	New York

Pack Your Bags Game

Pretend you are moving to one of the places above. Name one item you would pack, add a second item that begins with the last letter of the first item. Continue until you run out of things to add. Can be done as a six member team to see which team can complete six items first. [*Example*: jeans, socks, sweater, raincoat, toothbrush, handkerchief]

GOOD READING: PLACES IN THE WORLD

Berkes, Marianne. *Over in the Ocean.* Dawn Publications, 2004.
    Marine life introduced with music, math, and colorful art.

Brown, Don. *Far Beyond the Garden Gate.* Houghton-Mifflin, 2002.
    Alexandra David-Neel's journey through the wild Tibetan tablelands in 1934.

Collard, Sneed, III. *1000 Years Ago on Planet Earth.* Houghton-Mifflin, 1999.
    How people lived throughout the world 1,000 years ago.

Curlee, Lynn. *Into the Ice Age: The Story of Arctic Exploration.* Houghton-Mifflin, 1998.
    Stories of dangerous expeditions including a Dutch expedition who spent an entire winter in a driftwood shelter at 50 degrees below zero.

Jenkins, Steve. *Hottest, Coldest, Highest, Deepest.* Houghton-Mifflin, 1998.
    An introduction to geography done as a record book about places on the Earth.

Lewis, J. Patrick. *A World of Wonders.* Dial, 2002.
    Geographic travels in verse.

Martin, Jacqueline Briggs. *The Lamp, the Ice and the Boat Called* Fish. Houghton-Mifflin, 2001.
    In 1913, a boat called *Fish*, part of the Canadian Arctic Expedition, became stuck in the Arctic ice. The odds for survival of those aboard were not good.

Peters, Lisa. *Earthshake.* Greenwillow, 2003.
    A wonderful collection of poems about the Earth.

Pfetzer, Mark, and Jack Galvin. *Within Reach: My Everest Story.* Dutton, 1998.
    The personal story of the youngest climber ever to climb Everest.

Pringle, Laurence. *Global Warming: The Threat to the Earth's Changing Climate.* Sea Star, 2001.
    An introduction to an urgent environmental problem.

Rogers, Sally. *Earthsong.* Dutton, 1998.
    A song about endangered wildlife to foster awareness.

Rumford, James. *Traveling Man.* Houghton-Mifflin, 2001.
    A record of the 75,000 mile journey of Ibn Battuta in the 14th century.

Part Four

U.S. History

The fifer had a headache because . . .

U.S. HISTORY BOOK REVIEWS

A One Sentence-At-A-Time Report

Number of Players: Six

Objective: To demonstrate comprehension of a text by recreating a booktalk based on a historical incident. Tell six players that they are going to recreate a booktalk one sentence at a time.

Procedure: Six players retell one of the talks that follow. Give a copy to each player. Allow them time to read and then put aside the information. The players stand facing the group. The first player begins the review with one sentence. Each student in turn uses one sentence to continue the review. Challenge the group to see if it can retell the review in three or four rounds.

Follow Up: Use the same procedure to introduce books of any U.S. historical era. Team members can re-tell the jacket copy of the books.

THE PILGRIMS

The Serpent Never Sleeps by Scott O'Dell. Houghton-Mifflin, 1987.

Serena Lynn, age seventeen, is asked by England's King James I, to serve at court. She is very pleased, but must decline; she is loyal to the man she's always loved, Anthony Foxcroft. Anthony is embroiled in disputes at court and must ship out for Jamestown, the first colony in the New World, Serena will go too.

They sail on the Sea Venture, which leaves Plymouth, England in 1609 to take supplies and more settlers to Virginia. Their small boat seems no match for the wild sea, but they are spared—only to be shipwrecked off Bermuda. The brave crew builds a new boat so their expedition can flounder on to Virginia.

When they arrive, Jamestown is in ruins. Those who have survived the deadly winter are in desperate need of food. The Indians, with whom the colonists have maintained a delicate peace, may be their only chance. Serena goes with a party sent to plead with Pocahontas, the Indian princess who saved them once before, and who may have the power to save them again.

THE REVOLUTION

Haym Salomon, American Patriot by Susan Goldman Rubin. Abrams, 2007.

Haym Salomon was one of the few Jewish patriots of Revolutionary times. His knowledge of languages and currencies made him an exceptional man in pre-Revolution New York. Incredibly valuable to the revolutionary cause, Haym risked his life and his fortune, went to prison, and was forced to abandon his home and family, all for the sake of American independence.

Aaron and the Green Mountain Boys by Patricia Lee Gauch. Boyds Mill, 2005.

In the summer of 1777 the small town of Bennington, Vermont, was roused in the middle of the night. The British redcoats were on their way to take the supplies stored near Bennington. Nine-year-old Aaron Robinson pictured himself bravely running through lines with messages for the generals, or heroically guarding his grandfather's tavern, or even taking part in a battle with the Green Mountain Boys. Instead he was told to help his grandfather bake bread for the soldiers.

Johnny Tremain by Esther Forbes. Houghton-Mifflin, 1943.

Clever and gifted Johnny Tremain is apprenticed to a silversmith in the year 1773. Johnny sees a great future ahead until the day that carelessness caused his hand to be so badly burned that his dreams of being a silversmith were gone. Johnny becomes bitter and feels useless until he becomes a dispatch rider for the Committee of Public Safety and gets to know the leaders of the Revolution. With the rapid events that follow leading to independence, Johnny fills a valuable role in securing the nation's freedom from English oppression. Live through two years of history with Johnny Tremain and watch through his eyes as the revolution unfolds.

THE NATIONAL ANTHEM

By the Dawn's Early Light by Steven Kroll. Scholastic Hardcover, 1994. (Picture Book)

It was only days after the British had burned a defenseless Washington that Francis Scott Key learned that a good friend, Dr. William Beanes, was being held captive on board a British ship. Driven by devotion to his friend and his country, Key obtained presidential permission to visit the British fleet to request the release of Dr. Beanes. But to his horror, Key was forced to stay on board as the ship attacked Fort McHenry. From the deck of the enemy ship Key watched helplessly as the British bombed the American fort.

However, by the dawn's early light, the American flag was flying over the fort and Francis Scott Key was inspired to write the words to the song that became the National Anthem.

SLAVERY / CIVIL WAR

Which Way Freedom by Joyce Hansen. Walker & Company, 1985.

The slave traders herded Obie and Buka onto the boat. Buka kept his arm around the young Obie as the ship pulled away from the South Carolina coast. Inside his head Obie could still hear the screams of his mother as he was taken from her. "Look after my boy," she screamed to Buka. He tightened his grip on the shaking child and hung on to him all the way to the slave pen at the Charleston market. "Your mama's name is Lorena," he told Obie. "Don't forget now, her name is Lorena." Obie knew he would never forget and furthermore some day he would find his mama and take both of them to freedom. Little did Obie know *Which Way Freedom* lay!

Cassie's Sweet Berry Pie: A Civil War Story by Karen B. Winnick. Boyds Mill, 2005.

Cassie can't remember when she last tasted huckleberry pie. Ever since war broke out between the states, her life in Mississippi has changed. Her father is off fighting with General Lee's army. Her mother spends hours tending wounded soldiers at the hospital.

But when Cassie picks a bucket of huckleberries, her mother provides her with enough flour and sugar to make a pie. So, while keeping an eye on her younger brother and sister, Cassie cuts long strips of dough. Suddenly a neighbor brings word that Union soldiers are close by stealing food. Cassie and her siblings hurry to hide their pork, cheese, and sack of potatoes. Then Cassie gets an idea of how she might keep the Union soldiers from discovering her family's precious food. She proves that huckleberries are useful for more than just making pies.

Mr. Lincoln's Drummer Boy by G. Clifton Wisler. Scholastic, 1995. (Novel)

Willie enlisted in the Union Army at the age of eleven. He left his ma, two brothers, and the place he called home in Vermont, and boarded a train with his pa to fight in a war. Since he has learned to play drum rolls he knows his job will be to wake the troops in the morning as well as to carry out commands to advance or retreat in battle. The battles did not start immediately as Willie and Pa spend three months at Camp Griffin with little to occupy them. When the battles do begin, there is more suffering and death from the mosquito-ridden swamp in which they find themselves than from battle wounds. Working as a stretcher bearer as well as a drummer boy Willie becomes ill and after a brief meeting with President Lincoln he is sent to a hospital to recover. Eventually he receives the Congressional Medal of Honor for his valiant service during the battles known as "Seven Days." What an extraordinary accomplishment for an eleven-year-old!

SLAVERY

Escape From Slavery: Five Journeys To Freedom by Doreen Rappaport. Illustrated by Charles Lilly. HarperCollins, 1991.

Eliza was stunned to hear the master's words. She was to be sold and separated from her two-year-old daughter, Caroline. She knew what she had to do. Late that night she wrapped Caroline in a blanket and tiptoed out of the cabin, the night air biting her face. Through the night she walked in the icy air through the woods to the river . . . the river that separated the slave state of Kentucky from the free state of Ohio. The frozen ground bit through her thin shoes, yet the frozen river would be even colder and more dangerous to cross. Just before daylight she reached the river. The ice had broken up. She would have to hide and wait for the cold night wind to freeze the water once again. The baby cried out. "Shush," Eliza said. "The slave hunters will hear!" Then Eliza spotted a small cabin in the distance. She had heard that some colored folks who lived along the river would help runaways. She looked around, there was no other place to hide. Caroline would not survive the freezing cold for a day. The trackers would soon be there. Eliza had no way of knowing who lived in the cabin as she raised her hand and knocked gently on the door.

GOING WEST

Wagon Wheels by Barbara Brenner. HarperCollins, 1993. (Picture Book)

Wagon Wheels is based on a true story. In 1878, Ed Muldie left Kentucky with his family to go to Kansas. They had heard about the Homestead Act which promised free land to anyone willing to help settle the West. Many black pioneers like the Muldies settled in Kansas. The boys in this story stayed alone in a dugout and traveled 150 miles to find their father. The family faced starvation, freezing cold, rattlesnakes, wild animals, and prairie fires but survived it all to make a home on the prairie

Jericho's Journey by F. Clifton Wisler. Puffin Books, 1995. (Novel)

It was October 1852 and Jericho Wetherby and his family were finally on their way to Texas. Jericho had lived his whole life in County, Tennessee, never traveling more than fifty miles away from home. For years he had heard the stories his father had told about the battle of the Alamo and Texas winning independence from Mexico. Now, after all these exciting stories along with the letters Uncle Dan had written telling about the wonders of Texas, Jericho and his family along with Eli Grady, the cousin of a neighbor "up rover," were on their way to Texas.

Jericho knew winter would be setting in soon and time was of the essence, but traveling with one wagon, some animals, and three young boys on foot would be slow. Would they get to their new home in Texas before winter set in? What hardships would they have to endure on their trip through Tennessee and Arkansas?

Will Jericho and his family make it all the way to Texas or will they turn around and go home as so many others have done?

LEGENDARY HEROES

Pecos Bill by Steven Kellogg. Mulberry Books, 1986.

Raised by coyotes Pecos Bill grew up to be the greatest cowboy in Texas or anywhere else. Besides inventing lassoing, cattle roping, and rodeos, he could tame rattlesnakes, wrestle dangerous critters, and even make the terrible Hell's Gulch Gang turn respectable. But his two greatest feats were winning the hearts of Lightning and of Slewfoot Sue—the wildest horse and the wildest woman of the West.

THE RIVERS

Mike Fink retold and illus. by Steven Kellogg. Morrow, 1992.

Mike Fink, keelboat man was the most daring and rugged frontiersman on the river. A runaway at two days old, Mike grew up to be a king of the keelboatmen, the strong, rowdy men who floated cargo down river to New Orleans and poled heavy boats against the current.

But first Mike became a crackerjack marksman with his gun, Bang-All, then grappled with grizzlies. No man, alligator, or snapping turtle could last against the mighty Mike Fink. That is until Hilton P. Blathersby and his powerful smoke-spewing steamboat came along. Will Mike make it first to the finish line or will he lose his river crown?

NATIVE AMERICANS

Sing Down the Moon by Scott O'Dell. Houghton Mifflin, 1970.

The spring that came to the Canyon de Chelly in 1864 was abundant, for the fields and orchards of the Navajos who lived there promised a rich harvest. The sheep were lambing and the sky was bright blue. But all was shattered when the white soldiers burned the crops, destroyed the fruit trees, and forced the Navajos out of the canyon to join their brothers on the devastating long march to Fort Sumner. Through the eyes of Bright Morning, a young Navajo girl, we see what can happen to human beings when they are uprooted from the life they know. She tells the story of the proud and able Tall Boy, the youth she expected to marry, who is maimed not only by a physical wound, but a spiritual wound as well. And she tells of the other men of the tribe who on the march along the "Trail of Tears" lose their will along with their way of life. It is a story with tragic overtones, a story of the breaking of the human spirit. And yet, fortunately, then as now, there were a few possessed of inner strength based on hope; Bright Morning was one of these.

TO A NEW WORLD

Twist of Gold by Michael Morpurgo. Viking, 1993

Plague! First the pestilence that turned the potatoes in the ground to black spuds and now the fever upon the people. *Plague!* As soon as Sean O'Brien's friend whispers the word, Sean knows his last hope of staying in Ireland is gone. Leaving his mother, too wasted from famine to travel, in his friend's care, Sean and his sister Annie must now go in search of their father, to the strange land they know only from their father's letters, America.

Sean knows the journey will be hard. But he's overcome hardship before. What he doesn't expect is what will happen now that he carries the torch, the golden necklace of his ancestors and the symbol of his clan. The precious gold attracts a host of thieves, from the mercenary sea captain on Sean and Annie's nightmare crossing, to the slave hunter who tracks them across the west. But the torch, and the courage and cunning Sean and Annie show in protecting it, also earn the children new friends. Still, they need more than friends to survive the dangerous trek across America. They'll need all their determination and daring, and all the mysterious power of fate held in a twist of gold.

Wildflower Girl by Marita Conlon-McKenna. Illustrated by Donald Teskey. Holiday House, 1993.

Thirteen-year-old Peggy O'Driscoll can find no work in her small village in Ireland so she sets off on a terrifying voyage to America and arrives in the big city of Boston to find work as a maid to Mrs. Cavendish, a drunken landlady who runs a boarding house. Peggy is overworked and underfed. Then one night Mrs. Cavendish is missing and the men want their supper. Peggy finds only eggs to cook and fixes them for the men. Much later that night Peggy is awakened by blows from the landlady. She refuses to listen to Peggy's explanation for the missing eggs and beats the girl severely. Left alone with a bloody face and a missing tooth Peggy vows to run away. But where will she run to? Signs in every store window say "No Irish Need Apply." Anything would be better than this, Peggy thinks, as she carefully makes her way down the stairs and out the door.

HISTORY TOLD TWO WORDS AT A TIME

Number of Players: Individuals or partners.

Objective: To transform narrative into poetry.

Directions: Verla Kay had done several picture books where she recounts a historical incident, two to three words at a time, in poetry form. Study the poetry model below. Retell or rewrite any of the previous book reviews using the two-word-at-a-time poetry model.

Follow Up: Use the same procedure to retell any historical incident.

Mary Ludwig Hays McCauley (Molly Pitcher) 1754-1832
She fought beside the troops in the Revolutionary War

Cannons near	Bullet hit
Dangerous life	Husband fell
Molly Pitcher	Empty cannon
Caring wife	Battle yell
Husband fought	Molly lifted
Molly, too	cannon ball
Cleaning, mending	Into barrel
Cooking stew	Ramrod all
Battle raging	Loading cannon
Smoke-filled air	Exhausted, tired
Bullets whizzing	Ramrod pushed
Everywhere.	Cannon fired.
Molly moved	Molly Pitcher
without fear	Soldier's friend
Answering cries	Fired until
Over here!	Battle's end.

Good Reading: *Covered Wagons, Bumpy Trails*, 2000; *Homespun Sarah*, 2003; *Orphan Train*, 2003; *Iron Horses*, 2002; *Tattered Sails*, 2004. All by Verla Kay. All published by Putnam.

WHO SAID THAT?

Number of Players: Five to seven plus a leader.

Objective: To introduce well-known quotations. To create a story of historical fiction two or three sentences at a time.

Procedure: The group decides on a good title for a story. Each player in turn, tells the story with two or three sentences, one of which contains the quotation from the slip of paper he or she is holding. Each player, in turn, continues the story in the same way until the story is told. The story should be completed in no less than two or more than three rounds.

The Quotations

"When angry, count to ten before you speak." —*Thomas Jefferson*
"Give me liberty or give me death." —*Patrick Henry*
"I would rather be right than be President." —*Henry Clay*
"Laziness travels so slowly that poverty soon overtakes him." —*Benjamin Franklin*
"A little neglect may breed mischief." —*Benjamin Franklin*

Good Reading: *Let It Begin Here: Lexington and Concord* by Dennis Fradin. Walker, 2005; *The One and Only Declaration of Independence* by Judith St. George. Philomel, 2005.

MORE QUOTATIONS

"Nothing but money is sweeter than honey."
—*Benjamin Franklin*

"We must all hang together or we shall hang separately."
—*Benjamin Franklin*

"We have met the enemy and they are ours."
—*Commodore Perry*

"War is hell."
—*General Sherman*

"Don't fire until you see the whites of their eyes."
—*William Prescott at Bunker Hill*

"I came through and I shall return."
—*Douglas MacArthur*

"The only thing we have to fear is fear itself."
—*Franklin Roosevelt*

"The eyes of the world are upon you."
—*Dwight D. Eisenhower*

THE POETRY LINE STORY

Number of Players: Six or twelve.

Objective: To produce a story that includes poetry lines. The players will create a story two or three lines at a time. Each player will have one slip of paper containing a line from *The Landing of the Pilgrim Fathers* by Felicia Hemans. The player must work the poetry line into the story.

Procedure: The group decides on a good title for a story. Each player in turn, tells the story with two or three sentences, one of which contains the poetry line from the slip of paper he or she is holding. Each player, in turn, continues the story in the same way until the story is told. The story should be completed in no less than two or more than three rounds.

The Lines

The breaking of the waves dashed high
On a stern and rockbound coast
And the woods against a stormy sky
Their giant branches tossed
And the heavy night hung dark
The hills and water o'er
When a band of exiles moored their bark
On that storm-tossed Plymouth shore
The ocean eagle soared
From his nest by the white wave's foam
And the rocking pines of the forest roared
This was their welcome home

Good Reading: *Hour of Freedom: American History in Poetry* by Milton Meltzer. Boyds Mill, 2003.

TITLE STORIES: AMERICAN HISTORY

Number of Players: Teams of five or six.

Objective: Students will create a title and story using words from titles of historical fiction.

Procedure: Select teams of five or six players. Each team receives a list of six historical fiction titles. One word is to be chosen from four to six of the titles. The words are put together to form a new title. The form or tense of a word can be changed. The team then creates and tells a story related to the new title.

Example:

The Great **American** Goldrush

In the Eye of War

Straight Along a **Crooked** Road

Follow **the** Drinking Gourd

Which **Way** Freedom

Pioneer **Trailblazer**

> **Words Chosen**
> American
> crooked
> the
> way
> trailblazer

THE CROOKED AMERICAN TRAILBLAZER WAY

The Story

There was once a adventurous young fellow who couldn't walk straight. He was always getting lost because of the crooked trails he marked. He would find something interesting on a journey but could never find it again.

One day he found a big pot of gold right in the middle of the forest. It was too heavy to carry so he had to go back to his wagon to get some smaller sacks to put it in. As he weaved this way and that, he marked the trail with bread crumbs.

Returning to the trail the bread crumbs were gone. He walked and he walked but could not find the gold. He decided that the best way to get rich was to get a job, for he would never find gold the crooked American trailblazer way

HISTORY TITLES

The Buck Stops Here
Lily and Miss Liberty
Nettie's Trip South
The Last Princess
Kara's New World
Death of the Iron Horse
The Amazing, Impossible Erie Canal
Davy Crockett at the Alamo
From Sea to Shining Sea
No Hero for the Kaiser
Then What Happened Paul Revere?

MORE HISTORY TITLES

The Door in the Wall
Path of the Pale Horse
Wings Around the World
A Boy and His Bear
The House of Wisdom
Wish Me Luck
Star of Fear, Star of Hope
Circle of Fire
The Great Turkey Walk
Beyond the Divide
The Art of Keeping Cool

May be copied for classroom use. *From Get Up and Move with Nonfiction* by Nancy Polette. Westport, CT: Teacher Ideas Press. Copyright © 2008.

SEQUELS TO HISTORY

Number of Players: Two

Objective: To understand that every issue has two or more points of view.

Procedure: Each member of the audience writes a short 3-5 word phrase on a slip of paper. Phrases are placed face down on the floor or table. These phrases can be song titles, book titles, lines from favorite poems, proverbs, or simple statements such as "Have a good day," or "The moon is full tonight."

Two players will take part in one of the following scenarios. As the dialogue progresses, each player must pick up one of the slips of paper and use the phrase in his or her dialogue. The phrase must make sense given the context of the situation. The game ends when each player has used three of the phrases.

Scenario One

Stranded at Plimoth Plantation, 1626 by Gary Bowen. HarperCollins, 1994

13-year-old Chris is an indentured servant to his unscrupulous uncle, Captain Sibsey. The Sparrowhawk's crew set sail October 12 from London in hopes of reaching Jamestown. The ship carried 266 passengers, mostly Irish servants. On November 6 the ship crashed in a fog on what the Captain said was the New England shore. Chris discovers that they are stranded on Plimoth Plantation. He visits with the Indians, eats lobsters and pumpkins for the first time, drills with the militia, hunts, fishes, plants crops, and helps to build houses.

Two players take the parts of Chris and a new servant who has arrived on another ship. The new servant is appalled at the primitive conditions at Plimoth Plantation and expresses his fears. Chris tries to convince the new arrival that life in the New World can be exciting and rewarding.

Scenario Two

When Washington Crossed the Delaware by Lynne Cheney. Simon & Schuster, 2004.

Christmas night, 1776, was a troubled time for our young country. In the six months since the Declaration of Independence had been signed, General George Washington and his troops had suffered defeat after defeat at the hands of the British. It looked as though the struggle for independence might be doomed, when Washington made a bold decision. He would lead the main body of his army across the Delaware River and launch a surprise attack on enemy forces.

Washington and his men were going against the odds. It seemed impossible that the ragtag Americans could succeed against the mightiest power in the world. But the men who started across the icy Delaware loved their country and their leader. Under his command they hoped to turn the tide of battle.

Two players take the parts of two of Washington's men. They are in one of the boats crossing the Delaware on a freezing Christmas night. They have a conversation about their present circumstances and their hopes for the dangerous mission.

Scenario Three

Dangerous Crossing by Stephen Krensky. E. P. Dutton, 2005.

It is February 1778, the height of the Revolutionary War. The American representative from Massachusetts, John Adams, is sent on a secret mission to France. It is dangerous to cross the Atlantic Ocean in the middle of winter, but the situation is desperate, the colonies need France's help against the British army. Adams brings along his ten-year-old son, Johnny. Together Johnny and his father must weather an angry ocean, perilous sea battles, and other dangers to help the colonies reach freedom.

Two players take the part of Adams and his son during a terrible storm at sea. The son questions the purpose of the difficult voyage and Adams attempts to explain the importance of the trip.

Scenario Four

U.S. Kid's History: Book of the American Revolution by Howard Egger-Bovet and Marlene Smith-Barabzini. Little Brown, 1994.

By 1763 Great Britain has claimed most of what is now the United States and Canada by winning the French and Indian Wars. But then new trouble started, this time with their colonists. Through the colonists' hard work, the British were making a lot of money, far more than the colonists themselves. The British were also passing new laws that told the colonists what they could do and not do. The colonists began to wonder whether this was fair. They began to wonder who really owned the land they had settled.

Two players debate whether the British or the colonists should make the laws and levy taxes on the colonies. One player takes the British position. The other player feels the colonies should be free of British taxes and rule.

Scenario Five

Saving the Liberty Bell by Megan McDonald. Atheneum, 2005.

John Jacob Mickley, eleven years old, and his father were in Philadelphia in 1777 when the great Liberty Bell rang from atop the State House to warn the citizens that "The Redcoats are coming!"

And come the British did, with their muskets and their cannons and their will to keep the colonies for their king. Looting they came and stealing any metal they could get their hands on to melt down for the making of more weapons. And the prize above all? The Great Bell itself, metal for many a cannon. But the clever citizens of Philadelphia were determined that the British would not seize the bell. The huge bell weighed 2,080 pounds.

Two players discuss options for hiding the bell from the British. How and where can it be moved?

Scenario Six

Daniel Boone by James Daugherty. Viking, 1939. The award-winning tale of the farmer who couldn't stay put.

Daniel Boone was a farmer who couldn't stay put. Something was always pulling him westward into new and mysterious lands, and when this pull got so strong that he could no longer ignore it, and his wife could not persuade him to stay, he just went with his toes pointing west and his eyes glued into the hills. Read about the adventures of this early frontiersman in *Daniel Boone*.

Two players take the parts of Daniel Boone and his wife, Rebecca. Daniel is explaining to Rebecca why it is necessary for him to travel westward to new lands. Rebecca wants him to remain home on the farm.

Scenario Seven

A Dog Came, Too by Ainslie Manson. Illustrated by Ann Blades. McElderry Books, 1993.

In 1793, the explorer Alexander Mackenzie journeyed across Canada to the Pacific Ocean, the first European to cross North America. He and his party were accompanied by a big, brown dog and the men soon became fond of him. The faithful dog was a fine hunter and kept watch every night, scaring away wolves, bears, and other prowlers. Since there was no room for the dog in the canoes, he journeyed on foot all the way. When the explorers were near the Pacific Ocean they camped with friendly Indians. Our Dog went deep into the woods that night, found a dark cave, and slept soundly after many days of hard travel. The next day when Mackenzie and his party were ready to leave, Our Dog was missing and they continued without him. But Our Dog followed the river, hoping to find them. When the explorers started their return journey, they discovered him, weak and half-starved, waiting for them. All of this was recorded by Alexander Mackenzie in his journals, a touching true story about the first dog to cross the continent by land

Two players take the parts of Alexander Mackenzie and another member of the expedition when they discover the lost dog. They speculate on how the dog managed to survive.

STOP THE ACTION

Number of Players: One, plus a Tracker.

Objective: The player incorporates audience suggestions into the monologue.

The Scenario

In the days of slavery many slaves attempted to escape their bondage. Escape was not easy. It meant evading the trackers' dogs, hiding by day, and traveling at night in hope of finding a friendly house that would be the first step on the Underground Railroad journey.

Barefoot by Pamela Duncan Edwards. HarperCollins, 1997.
Under a cover of darkness, a Barefoot, an escaped slave, flees for his life. His captors are on his trail. He is terrified. And he sees no signs of the Underground Railroad, his road to freedom, because the moon is hidden by the clouds.

Then a frog croaks, leading the Barefoot to water. A mouse rustles where berries grow, and the Barefoot eats. A heron cries, warning of danger, for the Barefoot's captors are closing in. But as the captors walk through the tall grass, they disturb a swarm of mosquitoes and are attacked by the insects. The captors flee, following the sound of an escaping deer and the Barefoot finds himself safe and ready to travel again. Soon he comes upon a safe house and knows that he has taken the first steps to freedom; helped, of course, by the many wild creatures.

Procedure

The player takes the part of the slave telling of his/her experience. After the scene is well established the Tracker calls "FREEZE!" and asks the stranger for a reply to a question. The player must incorporate the reply in the dialogue. The game continues until the action has been frozen three times.

Sample questions the Tracker might ask:
- What are you holding in your hand?
- What is something you need that you don't have?
- Why do you have a black eye, bandaged arm, limp, etc.?
- What past experience with _____ have you had?
- How did you come to be in this place at this time?
- What is your greatest fear?

Good Reading: *Young Patriots* by Marcella Anderson and Elizabeth Vollstadt. Boyds Mill, 2004.

THE START AND THE FINISH

Number of Players: Teams of two.

Objective: Each team will create and act out a scene developed from two sentences.

Procedure: Each team receives a strip of paper with a beginning and ending sentence. The teams have five minutes to think of a scene that will fit the sentences. Each team acts out its scene using the beginning and ending sentence.

The old trapper was a doting fool of a father.   That was one of the reasons why it failed.
He would burst into storms of devilish temper without notice.   Enemies were in strong force here.
He had worn himself out tracking the animal.   He was considerably hurt, but not seriously.
This was the last feather.   The enemy was holed up like a rat in a trap.
Sleep would not come while the storm raged.   The blizzard had claimed its own.
She would burst into storms of devilish temper without notice.   It was a common trick.

Good Reading: *Blizzard of 1888* by Laura Francesca Filipucci. Walker, 2004.

THE SHORTEST POSSIBLE STORY

Number of Players: Teams of two or three.

Objective: To develop a storyline through associative thinking.

Procedure: Teams are given nonfiction book titles and are to use them in any order to create a short story.

If You Were There in 1776 Come All You Brave Soldiers The World Turned Upside Down
Yankee Doodle America, the Spirit of 1776 George Versus George Give Me Liberty!
Billy Yank and Johnny Reb Hold the Flag High The Silent Witness
The Boys' War The Long Road to Gettysburg United No More!

THE SHORTEST POSSIBLE NONFICTION ACCOUNT

Number of Players: Teams of two or three.

Objective: To develop a storyline through associative thinking.

Procedure: Teams are given three or more nonfiction facts. The sentences are not connected in any way. The team is to construct and tell the shortest possible story using the three sentences in any order.

The earliest bridges were fallen logs that helped a person cross a stream.

Baseball is considered the national game of the United States.

Penny, an English hen, broke a record by laying seven eggs in one day.

The famous race between a horse and a steam locomotive took place in 1830.

"Steamboat Willie" was the first cartoon with a sound track.

Devil's Tower is a volcanic rock in Wyoming 865 feet tall.

Joshua Pusey obtained a patent for book matches in 1892.

In 1974 a pogo stick jumping record was set at six hours and six minutes.

The great Chicago fire disaster occurred in 1871.

The circus known as "The Greatest Show on Earth" began in 1873.

The Pony Express stopped its mail service in 1861.

Artificial rain is created to drench a forest fire.

King Tutankhamen's tomb is discovered.

"Ma", a female tabby cat lives to the age of 34.

Electric power failure caused a 13 hour blackout in states in the Northeast.

THE ABCs OF HISTORY

Number of Players: Four to six.

Objective: The players will retell an incident from history with each sentence beginning with a consecutive letter of the alphabet.

Procedure: The team decides on the incident they will retell. Speaking in turn, each member of the team will help in the telling, one sentence or phrase at a time, but each must begin his or her sentence with the next letter of the alphabet. To make the game easier, each team member should know which letters he or she will be using before the telling starts, and think of as many words as he or she can that begin with those letters.

The Event: Remember the Alamo!

Besieged by Santa Anna at the Alamo in 1836, Colonel William Travis, with his force of 182, refused to surrender but elected to fight and die for the independence of Texas. Their requests for assistance had gone unheeded. As the Battle of the Alamo was in progress a small band of 32 men made their way through the enemy lines and joined the doomed defenders and perished with them.

Realizing that Santa Anna and his 4,000 strong army would soon take the Alamo, Travis addressed his men, told them that they were fated to die for the cause of liberty and the freedom of Texas. He gave them the option of leaving if they could. None did.

A breech in the palisades allowed the enemy to enter and the fate of the defenders was death. They faced it bravely, asking no quarter and giving none. The siege of the Alamo ended on the dawn of March 6, when its gallant defenders were put to the sword.

The women and children in the Mission were spared. But it was not an idle sacrifice that men like Travis and Davy Crockett and James Bowie made at the Alamo. It was a sacrifice on the altar of liberty that later spurred on the forces of Sam Houston at San Jacinto the cry of "Remember the Alamo!"

Good Reading: *Susanna of the Alamo* by John Jakes. Harcourt, 1986.

THE ABCs OF HISTORY

More Incidents to Retell

Show your understanding of the following passage by retelling or rewriting it as an ABC account with each line beginning with a letter of the alphabet.

The Great Molasses Flood of 1919

It was an unusually warm day for January 19, 1919 in Boston, Massachusetts. Little Jimmy DiStasio was on his way to the North End playground.

Looming over Commercial Street was a 58 foot high molasses tank owned by the Purity Distilling Company. The tank had been there for years. Those who worked on the street below paid little attention to it, not those in the Public Works Department building, or the men of Fire Boat 21 or those who worked in the freight sheds along the water front.

In one brief moment, all their lives were changed. A dull muffed roar gave but an instant's warning before the top of the tank was blown into the air. Two million gallons of molasses rushed over the streets, the sticky mass smashing several small buildings. One section of the tank fell on the nearby firehouse. The building was crushed and three firemen buried in the ruins. Two and one half million gallons of hot, sticky, smelly molasses covered the streets like a tidal wave moving at an incredible speed of 35 miles per hour. Wagons, carts, and motor trucks were overturned. An elevated train was lifted off the rails. A number of horses were killed.

The first rescue party on the scene was a squad detailed from the ship, Nantucket. The enlisted men tried to give first aid to the more than 150 injured and patrol the district but often found themselves stuck fast in the goo.

Twenty-two bodies were taken to a makeshift morgue at the end of Commercial Street where frantic relatives gathered. Jimmy's mother was among them. As she walked down the line of covered shapes, she stopped at one of the small, quiet mounds and lifted the cover and screamed. Underneath lay Jimmy. Her scream woke him up. "Mama," he said. Jimmy was one of the few in its path who had survived the Great Molasses Flood.

The next day, in an attempt to clean up the gooey mess, firemen used water hoses to pump water from the harbor; but the salt water made the molasses froth up, yellow and sudsy. Clean up would take weeks!

Information from *The New York Times*, January 20, 1919.

THE ABCs OF HISTORY

More Incidents to Retell

Show your understanding of the following passage by re-telling or re-writing it as an ABC account with each line beginning with a letter of the alphabet.

The Great Chicago Fire

It had been an extremely dry summer in Chicago when on October 8, 1871, legend tells that Mrs. O'Leary's cow kicked over a lantern in the cow shed and started the Great Chicago fire which lasted three days. No one knows for sure why the fire spread so quickly. Some say that Mrs. O'Leary waited too long to call for help. When her cries were heard, Mr. Lee, a neighbor, ignored the closest call box when running to report the fire. Mr. Brown a fire watcher, was playing cards when he should have been watching from a tower for any fires that might start in the city. When help did arrive it was a group of tired firemen, with equipment that needed repair, who had been fighting a different blaze most of the previous night.

Regardless of the reason the fire spread so quickly, it killed 250 people and destroyed 90,000 homes over an area of four square miles.

Good Reading: *The Great Fire* by Jim Murphy. Scholastic, 1995; *America's Great Disasters* by Martin Sandler. HarperCollins, 2003.

CHANGE OF MOOD

Number of Players: Seven

Objective: To see and imitate a mood. To be introduced to some of history's daredevils.

Procedure: Players take the parts of a mother and two children and one or more daredevils. They are seated as if on a train in two rows of two chairs, one row behind the other. Across the "aisle" is an empty chair.

Each new passenger occupies the empty chair, he begins a conversation with the players and must maintain one mood (happy, scared, sad, nervous, etc.) As soon as a player detects the mood that player must respond in the same mood. When all players are reflecting the passenger's mood, the passenger leaves and a new passenger arrives. The new passenger will reflect a different mood which players try to guess and reflect in their own speech and actions.

Passenger #1 is Evel Knievel, who jumps motorcycles over cars, trucks, and sharks. He is on his way to the Grand Canyon and is somewhat nervous about making his next jump (over the canyon). To date he has broken 33 bones. The players next to him and behind him are interested in hearing about his jumps.

Passenger #2 is Chuck Yeager, whose dangerous job as a test pilot included breaking the sound barrier in his plane the *Bell X-1*, at 670 miles per hour. Many test pilots before him tried to break the sound barrier and were killed in crashes and mid-air explosions. He is going home to celebrate his accomplishment with his family.

Passenger #3 is one of Kurt Wallenda's sons and a member of the circus wire-walking troop of the Flying Wallendas. The members of the troop walk without a net below, not only at the circus but between skyscrapers in New York City. The son is on his way to his father's funeral. Kurt Wallenda was killed in a high wire fall.

Good Reading: *Chuck Yeager Breaks the Sound Barrier* by Conrad Stein. Children's Press, 1997.

POINT OF VIEW

Number of Players: Four

Objective: Students will understand that opinions differ depending on individual circumstances.

Procedure: Individual players will take the parts indicated in the scenarios that follow and explain their points of view on the topic under discussion.

1. In 1825 the Erie Canal opened.

The first boat left Buffalo on October 26 and reached New York City November 4. Shortly after the completion of the canal, light packet boats, drawn by frequent relays of horses driven at a trot along the towpath, were making the trip between the Hudson River and Buffalo in three and a half days. The cost of construction was about $7,144,000, as well as the lives of many workers on the canal.

How do you feel about the completion of the Erie Canal?

A. The Mayor of New York City.

B. A homeowner whose land was taken to make room for the canal.

C. A business person in Buffalo who wants to sell goods to New Yorkers.

D. A widow of a worker who died while building the canal.

2. Railroad Crosses the Nation.

On July 1, 1862, President Abraham Lincoln signed the Pacific Railroad Act, which authorized the building and operation of a railroad between Sacramento, California, and the Missouri River. This was the beginning of the first transcontinental railroad, which was completed at Promontory Point, Utah, on May 10, 1869.

Was the coming of the railroad across country a good thing?

A. The owners of the railroad.

B. The Native Americans across whose lands the tracks would be laid.

C. The farmer.

D. A typical passenger.

(Continued)

Good Reading: *The Amazing, Impossible Erie Canal* by Cheryl Harness. Simon & Schuster, 1999; *Hear that Train Whistle Blow* by Milton Meltzer. Random House, 2004

3. Sound Barrier Broken by Supersonic Jet.

In 1947 the sound barrier was broken by Chuck Yeager in a rocket-powered aircraft. His supersonic jet flew 42,000 feet above the earth and reached a speed of 670 miles per hour. At the breaking of the sound barrier, a sonic boom was heard and felt in many homes. The shaking caused damage in some.

How do YOU feel about supersonic flight?

    A. Chuck Yeager, the test pilot.

    B. A General in the U.S. Air Force.

    C. The owner of a commercial airline.

    D. The homeowner who had cracks in walls due to the sonic boom.

4. First McDonald's Hamburgers Served in 1955.

Ray A. Kroc, who began the McDonald's chain, served hamburgers in his restaurant outside Chicago in 1955. Ten years later McDonald's had over 4,600 restaurants in 23 different countries.

Should you make a fast food restaurant your restaurant of choice?

    A. A high school football team member after a big game.

    B. A preschooler who likes the restaurant playground.

    C. A nutritionist.

    D. The owner of the fast food restaurant.

5. Speed Limit Lowered in 1973.

The speed limit was lowered from 70 miles per hour to 55 miles per hour, saving many lives as well as 2.4 billion gallons of gasoline every year. The speed limit for rural roads increased to 65 miles per hour. In the 1990s, most states again raised the speed limit to 70 miles per hour on interstates.

Should the speed limit be lowered once again?

    A. A state highway patrolman.

    B. The owner of a gas station.

    C. An emergency room doctor.

    D. A teenage driver.

Good Reading: *The Explorer's Handbook* by Marilyn Tolhurst. Dutton, 1998.

MIXED UP HISTORY

Number of Players: Teams of two.

Objective: To combine historical events into a single story.

Procedure: A team will choose three events in any row from the Tic Tac Tale board. After reading about the events, the team will combine facts from the events into a single story. The story can be told orally and then written.

BOSTON TEA PARTY	THE ALAMO	JOHNSTOWN FLOOD
SPIRIT OF ST LOUIS	PAUL REVERE'S RIDE	PONY EXPRESS
TRANSCONTINENTAL RAILROAD	SAN FRANCISCO EARTHQUAKE	ELLIS ISLAND

Example:

There was once a young fellow who wanted to imitate the famous ride of **Paul Revere.** However, instead of warning people about the British, he wanted to warn them about a crack in the dam above **Johnstown, PA.** He made the ride on May 30, 1889, telling folks to leave their homes since the heavy rains were putting too much pressure on the dam. "It will break any minute!" he shouted. But no one listened to him and the dam did break and washed away the town. If some of the track from the **transcontinental railroad** had been laid there the track would have washed away, too. But fortunately none of the track went through Johnstown so the railroad was built and the east and west tracks met in Utah 20 years later. By the way, Young Paul heeded his own warnings and left Johnstown to become the engineer of the first train to go coast to coast.

May be copied for classroom use. *From Get Up and Move with Nonfiction* by Nancy Polette. Westport, CT: Teacher Ideas Press. Copyright © 2008.

BOSTON TEA PARTY

On December 16, 1773 about 50 members of the political organization, The Sons of Liberty, boarded 3 ships in Boston Harbor. Some were dressed, not very convincingly, as Mohawk Indians. In a very orderly and quiet fashion, they plunked 9,659 [sterling] worth of Darjeeling tea into the sea.

The Boston Tea Party was a protest of British tax policies. It came in the midst of a boycott of English tea during which the East India Company, which owned the tea, had seen its profits plummet in the wake of a boycott of tea in the colonies. Consumption in the colonies had fallen from 900,000 lbs. in 1769 to 237,000 lbs. just 3 years later.

Good Reading: *The Boston Tea Party* by Pamela Duncan Edwards. Putnam, 2001.

PAUL REVERE'S RIDE

Revere confronted 2 British regulars manning a road block as he headed north across Charlestown Neck. As he turned around, the regulars gave chase and he eluded them. He then continued on to Lexington, to the home of Jonas Clarke where Sam Adams and John Hancock were staying. There, his primary mission was fulfilled when he notified Adams and Hancock that "The Regulars (British) are coming out!"

Revere and Dawes then headed for Concord and came across Doctor Prescott who then joined them. They decided to alarm every house along the way. Just outside of the town of Lincoln, they were confronted by four Regulars (British soldiers) at another road block. They tried unsuccessfully to run their horses through them. Prescott, who was familiar with the terrain, jumped a stone wall and escaped. Revere and Dawes tried to escape but shortly into the chase they were confronted by six more Regulars on horseback. Revere was surrounded and taken prisoner

The Regulars had Revere remount his horse and they headed toward Lexington Green, when suddenly, they heard a gunshot! The British officers then talked urgently among themselves and decided to release their captives so that they would not slow their retreat.

Good Reading: *Which Way to the Revolution?* by Bob Barner. Holiday House, 1998.

THE PONY EXPRESS

From 1860 to 1861 Pony Express riders delivered mail from Sacramento, California to St. Joseph, Missouri. An ad in a California newspaper read: "Wanted. Young, skinny, wiry fellows. Not over 18. Must be expert riders. Willing to risk death daily. Orphans preferred." Most riders were around 20. Youngest was 11. Oldest was mid-40s. Not many were orphans. Usually weighed around 120 pounds. The 2,000 mile run was done in less than ten days by a series of riders who changed horses every fifteen miles. There were many dangers on the trail ranging from a lack of water, rattlesnakes, bandits, and hostile Indians.

Good Reading: *Buffalo Bill and the Pony Express* by Eleanor Coerr. Harper Collins, 1998.

THE ALAMO

In 1836 the Mission known as the Alamo, became the "cradle of Texas Liberty." Rebelling against repressions of Mexico's self-proclaimed dictator, Santa Anna, a band of 182 Texas volunteers defied a Mexican army of six thousand for 13 days of siege from February 23 to March 6. The Alamo defenders died to the last man, among them such famous names as William Travis, Davy Crockett, and Jim Bowie. The cost to Mexican forces was dreadful. While Santa Anna dictated an announcement of glorious victory, his aide, Col. Juan Almonte, privately noted: "One more such glorious victory and we are finished." The finish came April 21 when Sam Houston's Texans routed the Mexican army at the Battle of San Jacinto near Houston.

Good Reading: *Voices of the Alamo* by Sherry Garland. Scholastic, 2000.

THE TRANSCONTINENTAL RAILROAD

The idea of a transcontinental railroad across North America was first seriously pursued by the head engineer of the Sacramento Valley Railroad. One of the most difficult problems facing him was crossing the Sierra Nevada mountains. The Rockies had several relatively easy passes through it. The Sierra Nevadas were consistently relentless, however. Finally he came up with a route through the mountains.

In 1869 two railroads were joined at Promontory, Utah. The building of track for the Union Pacific and the Central Pacific railroads was accomplished at a heavy cost of lives and money. Many said it could not be done but on May 10th when the tracks were complete, a golden spike was driven in celebration and for the first time it became possible to travel the entire United States, east to west coast, by train.

Good Reading: *Iron Horses* by Verla Kay. Putnam, 2002.

THE SAN FRANCISCO EARTHQUAKE

One of the most devastating earthquakes in history hit San Francisco in 1906. At almost precisely 5:12 a.m., local time, a foreshock occurred with sufficient force to be felt widely throughout the San Francisco Bay area. The great earthquake broke loose some 20 to 25 seconds later, with an epicenter near San Francisco. The tremors were so strong that buildings collapsed and the entire city caught fire. Smoke and dust were so thick that it was impossible to see. After several days when the fires showed no sign of abating, large areas were dynamited to prevent the fires from spreading. Thousands were left homeless. The frequently quoted value of 700 deaths caused by the earthquake and fire is now believed to underestimate the total loss of life by a factor of 3 or 4. Most of the fatalities occurred in San Francisco, and 189 were reported elsewhere.

Good Reading: *Earthquake* by Milly Lee. DK, 2001 (Picture Book); *Earthquakes* by Seymour Simon. Mulberry, 1995. (Nonfiction)

ELLIS ISLAND

During its peak years, 1892 to 1924, Ellis Island received thousands of immigrants a day. Each was scrutinized for disease or disability as the long line of hopeful new arrivals made their way up the steep stairs to the great, echoing Registry Room. Over 100 million Americans can trace their ancestry in the United States to a man, woman, or child whose name passed from a steamship manifest sheet to an inspector's record book in the great Registry Room at Ellis Island. With restrictions on immigration in the 1920s Ellis Island's population dwindled, and the station finally closed its doors in 1954.

Good Reading: *If Your Name Was Changed at Ellis Island* by Ellen Levine. Scholastic Hardcover, 1992.

SPIRIT OF ST. LOUIS

On May 21, 1927, Charles A. Lindbergh completed the first solo nonstop transatlantic flight in history, flying his Ryan NYP "Spirit of St. Louis" 5,810 kilometers (3,610 miles) between Roosevelt Field on Long Island, New York, and Paris, France, in 33 hours, 30 minutes. With this flight, Lindbergh won the $25,000 prize offered by New York hotel owner Raymond Orteig to the first aviator to fly an aircraft directly across the Atlantic between New York and Paris. When he landed at Le Bourget Field in Paris, Lindbergh became a world hero who would remain in the public eye for decades.

Reading: *Barnstormers and Daredevils* by K.C. Tessendorf. Atheneum, 1988.

THE JOHNSTOWN FLOOD

The New York Times, May 31, 1889.

A dam at the foot of a mountain lake eight miles long and three miles wide, broke at 4 o'clock on May 31, 1889. A tremendous volume of water swept in down the mountain side, making its own channel until it reached the South Fork of the Conemaugh, swelling it to the proportions of Niagara's rapids.

The flood swept onward like a tidal wave, over twenty feet in height, to Johnstown, six or eight miles below, gathering force as it tore along through the wider channel, and quickly swept everything before it. Houses, factories, and bridges were overwhelmed in the twinkling of an eye and with their human occupants were carried in a vast chaos down the raging torrent.

The water began flowing over the dam at about 1 o'clock, when Johnstown and people down the valley were warned by messengers to look out for a flood. Three hours later the whole end of the lake gave way, sweeping everything before it, including railroads, bridges, and telegraph lines.

The scene of the disaster was cut off from communication and details of the extent of the calamity were not immediately known. One telegraph operator says he counted sixty-three bodies in twenty minutes floating past his office.

Good Reading: *The Day It Rained Forever: The Story of the Johnstown Flood* by Virginia T. Gross. Puffin Books, 1999.

ONLY ONE!

Number of Players: Two

Objective: To demonstrate comprehension of a historical event by retelling the event using an "Only One" pattern.

Procedure: Two players are given a copy of one of the historical events on the previous three pages. Taking turns, each player retells the event by including "Only One" phrases in the telling.

Example:

ELLIS ISLAND

In the 1880s many immigrants wanted to come to the United States but there was **only one** way to enter.

Immigrants left behind many possessions for they were allowed to take **only one** bundle of belongings.

The ocean crossing was difficult, for the immigrants were kept in **only one** area, below decks.

There were many ports of entry for ships but **only one,** Ellis Island, for immigrant ships.

Thousands of immigrants had to stand in **only one** line.

The line was long because there was **only one** registry room.

Each immigrant had to pass **only one** physical examination.

In any family **only one** might be refused admittance because of poor health.

Immigrants felt the United States was the **only one** country where they could succeed at whatever they tried.

Good Reading: *Tattered Sails* by Verla Kay. Putnam, 2001.

WHOSE TALE IS TRUE?

Davy Crockett, 1786-1836

Reading Parts: Host, Davy Crockett #1, Davy Crockett #2, Davy Crockett #3

Host: Welcome to "Whose Tale Is True?" Each of our three guests claims to be Davy Crockett, hero, warrior, and backwoods statesman. Only one, however, is telling the complete truth. It is up to you to decide who the real Davy Crockett is. Now let's meet our guests. Welcome. We have all heard many legends about you. Did you really kill a bear when you were three years old?

Davy #1: No, I didn't. Folks just like to make up silly stories like that. Of course there were bears around the small cabin where I was born in 1786, the fifth son born to my folks John and Rebecca Crockett. If my pa saw a bear he most likely shot it and we had bear meat for supper. We mostly lived on whatever the land provided.

Davy #2: On the early frontier there were lots of bears but it was more likely a bear would kill a small child rather than the other way around. While I was still in dresses my pa moved the family to Cove Creek, Tennessee where he built a mill. When I was eight years old, the mill was washed away in a flood.

Davy #3: That's right. We then moved to Jefferson County where Pa built and operated a tavern. The tales I heard travelers tell sparked my desire for adventure. I only had four days of schooling, had a fight, and left home to escape a licking from my Pa. I got a job helping to drive cattle to Virginia.

Host: Tell us about your later adventures.

Davy #1: In my teens I worked to pay off some of my father's debts since I was the only son and my sisters were too young. I saved money to buy a rifle and horse.

Davy #2: When I was 20 I married and had two sons. A few years later I fought in the Indian Creek War and served as a Tennessee legislator and, for a brief time, as a member of the United States Congress.

Davy #3: Even though I had a lot of schooling I didn't take much to being a statesman. I much preferred life in the wild.

Host: What led you to the Alamo?

Davy #1: We got word that just a few men were holding off Santa Anna's army. Thought we might be of some help.

Davy #2: It was only right that my Tennessee Volunteers answered the call for help.

Davy #3: We were outnumbered 4,000 to 182, the end was inevitable but the fight for Texans to be free was worth it.

Host: Now it is time to decide whose tale is true. We will vote by a show of hands. Is it #1? Is it #2? Is it #3? Now for the moment you have all been waiting for. Will the real Davy Crockett step forward.

Answer: Davy #2

Good Reading: *Davy Crockett* by Larry Dane Brimner. Compass Point Books, 2004.

WHOSE TALE IS TRUE?

William F. Cody (Buffalo Bill), 1846-1917

Reading Parts: Host, Buffalo Bill #1, Buffalo Bill #2, Buffalo Bill #3

Host: Welcome to "Whose Tale Is True?" Each of our three guests claims to be Buffalo Bill, spokesman for the New West. Only one, however, is telling the complete truth. It is up to you to decide who the real Buffalo Bill is. Now let's meet our guests. Welcome. You have been described as a trapper, a bushwhacker, a "Fifty-Niner," a Pony Express Rider, a wagonmaster, stagecoach driver, and Civil War soldier. Is all of this true?

Buffalo Bill #1: Sure is! At age 11 I went to work for a freight firm that later became the Pony Express. That led to a time as a horse wrangler, hunter, and Indian fighter. I was one of the first riders for the Pony Express and rode for them for five years.

Buffalo Bill #2: After serving in the Civil War I worked for the U.S. Army as a scout and hunted buffalo to feed workers on the Kansas Pacific Railroad. In eight months I slaughtered 4,280 head of buffalo.

Buffalo Bill #3: For my work as a scout I was awarded the Medal of Honor in 1872 but later they took it away since I didn't hold any army rank. The Fifth Cavalry always asked for me to scout for them. They considered me good luck.

Host: How did you feel about becoming so famous?

Buffalo Bill #1: I never thought about fame during my one year with the Pony Express. It took ten days to make the 1,800 mile run from St. Joseph to Sacramento. No one man could ride all that way. I was part of a team.

Buffalo Bill #2: I never thought I did anything special. I just did my job. During my time as an army scout I was engaged in sixteen Indian fights and never got a scratch. Newspaper reporters played this up big and lots of stories were written about me that aren't true.

Buffalo Bill #3: I figured I could cash in on my fame and appeared on stage playing myself in "Scouts of the Prairie." I acted in the winter time and continued to scout for the Fifth Cavalry in the summer.

Host: Tell us about your Wild West Show.

Buffalo Bill #1: I started my own Wild West show in Omaha in 1883. It featured a buffalo hunt, a stagecoach robbery, cowboys and Indians, and a Pony Express Ride.

Buffalo Bill #2: I opened the show by riding around the ring in a fancy white get-up. I never would have worn that outfit as a scout. In one Indian fight I got a scalp wound. It would have been worse if I'd been dressed in my show outfit. I would have stuck out like a lantern in the dark.

Buffalo Bill #3: The Wild West Show was so popular that we were asked to perform at Queen Victoria's Golden Jubilee. Along with myself the show featured Annie Oakley and Chief Sitting Bull. I lost my fortune but I used my fame as a soapbox for the rights of Indians. America was the Indian's heritage and the Indian fought only for what was his.

Host: Now it is time to decide whose tale is true. We will vote by a show of hands. Is it #1? Is it #2? Is it #3? Now for the moment you have all been waiting for. Will the real William F. Cody step forward.

Answer: Buffalo Bill #3

Good Reading: *Buffalo Bill and the Pony Express* by Eleanor Coerr. HarperCollins, 1995.

WHOSE TALE IS TRUE?

Annie Oakley (Phoebe Ann Moses), 1860-1926

Reading Parts: Host, Annie Oakley #1, Annie Oakley #2, Annie Oakley #3

Host: Welcome to "Whose Tale Is True?" Each of our three guests claims to be Annie Oakley, world famous sharpshooter. Only one, however, is telling the complete truth. It is up to you to decide who the real Annie Oakley is. Now let's meet our guests. Welcome. I understand that you learned to handle a gun at a very early age.

Annie Oakley #1: That is true. I was born in a log cabin in the Ohio wilderness. We were very poor. My father died when I was five years old. I had eight brothers and sisters to be fed so I took my father's gun and headed for the woods.

Annie Oakley #2: I got to be a pretty good shot. There would not have been much to eat otherwise. My family was very poor. What little money we had I got by selling extra meat to the store.

Annie Oakley #3: When I was fifteen I entered my first shooting contest. I competed against Frank Butler, a champion shooter, and won by one shot. Frank didn't mind. In fact, a few years later we got married.

Host: Did you give up shooting contests after you were married?

Annie Oakley #1: Oh, no. Frank and I entered many contests together. I continued to send my prize money home to help my mother feed my six brothers and sisters. Frank and I gave lots of shooting demonstrations. Crowds really went wild when I shot a cigarette out of Frank's mouth.

Annie Oakley #2: Buffalo Bill offered me a part in his show. He thought I needed a catchy name. Since my family were Quakers and I liked Quaker Oats for breakfast I named myself Annie Oakley.

Annie Oakley #3: I traveled with Buffalo Bill's Wild West Show for seventeen years. I could shoot a dime tossed in the air. I could hit the thin edge of a playing card standing 90 feet away. I was always tiny, five feet tall. Folks wondered how I could enter the arena waving that heavy rifle in the air.

Host: Was it true that a train wreck cut your career short?

Annie Oakley #1: Yes. I was badly injured in a train week in 1901 when I was forty-one years old. For a time I was partly paralyzed and thought I would never perform again.

Annie Oakley #2: I was badly injured but I couldn't let the folks in Oakley, Ohio down. After all, I took my stage name after that town. I worked hard to recover and my shooting was as good as ever.

Annie Oakley #3: After the accident I didn't tour as much but I continued to enter shooting contests. I also trained soldiers to shoot during World War One. At age sixty-two I shot 100 clay pigeons without missing.

Host: Now it is time to decide whose tale is true. We will vote by a show of hands. Is it #1? Is it #2? Is it #3? Now for the moment you have all been waiting for. Will the real Annie Oakley step forward.

Answer: #3. #1 contradicted herself on the number of her brothers and sisters. #2 contradicted herself on how she chose her stage name.

Good Reading: *Shooting for the Moon: The Amazing Life and Times of Annie Oakley* by Stephen Krensky. Melanie Kroupa Books, New York, 2001; *Annie Oakley* by Frances Ruffin. Powerkids Press, New York, 2002.

WHOSE TALE IS TRUE?

Clara Barton, 1821-1912

Reading Parts: Host, Clara Barton #1, Clara Barton #2, Clara Barton #3

Host: Welcome to "Whose Tale Is True?" Each of our three guests claims to be Clara Barton, the battlefield nurse who founded the American Red Cross. Only one, however, is telling the complete truth. It is up to you to decide who the real Clara Barton is. Now let's meet our guests. Welcome. You must be a real go-getter to have accomplished as much as you have.

Clara Barton #1: My parents would laugh to hear you say that. I have always been painfully shy. When I was born in 1821 I was the youngest of five children. My mother used to worry because I was such a shrinking violet. As a young woman I had no formal training as a nurse, but nursed my ill brother for two years.

Clara Barton #2: I did not attend school but was educated at home. When I was fifteen years old I took a teaching job in New Jersey. I commuted by bus from my home to the school. I saw many children whose parents could not afford to send them to a private school so I started a free public school.

Clara Barton #3: By the time I was forty years old I had a job in the Patent Office in Washington, D.C. This was a terrible time for the nation when the North and South went to war. In working in the nation's capitol I became aware of the desperate need for medical supplies for our troops.

Host: Is that how you became known as a battlefield nurse?

Clara Barton #1: Because I was trained as a nurse I saw my job as getting the medical supplies to where they were needed. Once I arrived at the battlefields with wagons of supplies I saw the terrible shortage of medical people. I did what I could to help.

Clara Barton #2: I was so successful in getting supplies where they were needed that I was granted a pass to travel with the ambulances. Sometimes I had to bully men along the way to get help to the battlefields.

Clara Barton #3: I tended the wounded at Antietam, Manassas and Fredericksburg. After the war I headed a bureau to search for missing men. We were able to identify 12,000 men who died at Andersonville.

Host: How did the American Red Cross come about?

Clara Barton #1: In 1869 I went to Switzerland to serve as a nurse during the Franco-Prussian War. I saw the fine work that was being done there by the International Red Cross of Europe.

Clara Barton #2: I was determined that the United States should take part in the Red Cross work. The government refused to listen to my pleas until the Geneva Treaty was signed in 1882.

Clara Barton #3: The American Red Cross was established and I became its first president. It was my idea to extend Red Cross services to any group of people who face calamity. One of our first civilian efforts was helping those caught in the Jamestown flood in 1889.

Host: Now it is time to decide whose tale is true. We will vote by a show of hands. Is it #1? Is it #2? Is it #3? Now for the moment you have all been waiting for. Will the real Clara Barton step forward.

Answer: #3

Good Reading: *Clara Barton & Her Victory Over Fear* by Robert Quackenbush. Simon & Schuster, 1995.

WHOSE TALE IS TRUE?

Calamity Jane (Martha Jane Canary), 1852-1903

Reading Parts: Host, Calamity Jane #1, Calamity Jane #2, Calamity Jane #3

Host: Welcome to "Whose Tale Is True?" Each of our three guests claims to be Calamity Jane, the "Wild Devil of the Yellowstone." Only one, however, is telling the complete truth. It is up to you to decide who the real Calamity Jane is. Now let's meet our guests. Welcome. I read that you were born in Missouri. How did you end up in the Wild West?

Calamity Jane #1: Yes, I was born in Princeton, Missouri in 1852. When my mother died my Pa and brothers decided to try to strike it rich in the silver mines near Virginia City. That was when the first calamity happened.

Calamity Jane #2: The Indians didn't like the settlers moving onto their land and I was separated from my father and brothers in an Indian uprising. I was ten years old and there was nobody to phone back East to come and get me so I was on my own.

Calamity Jane #3: For the next ten years I got by as best I could. Having no mother to guide me, I wore men's clothing, chewed tobacco, and learned to be a pretty good shot. I could never stay in one place very long. For forty years I traveled from Arizona through the Dakota Territories.

Host: Is it true that you were a scout for the United States Army?

Calamity Jane #1: It sure is. When I was near twenty years old General Cook appointed me a scout. I was willing to go places others were afraid to go. Wild Bill Hickok was my boss. He knew I was up to any challenge. I think it's kind of nice that our final resting places are near each other in Deadwood, South Dakota.

Calamity Jane #2: It was while I was an army scout that I got my nickname. I was scouting in South Dakota when my Captain was surrounded by Indians. Captain Egan was wounded and had fallen off his horse. I rode in, picked him up, and got out of there. He's the one who named me Calamity Jane.

Calamity Jane #3: I really didn't think the name, Calamity, fit. I not only saved Captain Egan, but I saved six passengers in a runaway stage coach traveling from Deadwood to Wild Birch. The driver was wounded and the coach was out of control. I jumped from my horse to the driver's seat and got things under control.

Host: I think the folks in Deadwood, South Dakota would not call you Calamity, would they?

Calamity Jane #1: Probably not. You see, when I arrived there they were in the middle of a smallpox epidemic. I did what I could to help. The folks were so grateful that a few years later they wanted to have a big party to honor me but by that time I was at my final resting place in Arizona.

Calamity Jane #2: I was a Pony Express rider for a time and my route ran fifty miles from Deadwood to Custer. The Deadwood folks knew their mail would get through because robbers along the trail knew I was a crack shot. There were no calamities when I carried the mail.

Calamity Jane #3: When Wild Bill Hickok wrote about me he said I was remembered as a "saint" by the folks in Deadwood because of my help during the smallpox epidemic. Most folks would laugh at that idea. I was a rough riding, rough talking woman, and as good a shot as any man. I went where I pleased and did what I pleased and maybe along the line I did help a few folks out.

Host: Now it is time to decide whose tale is true. We will vote by a show of hands. Is it #1? Is it #2? Is it #3? Now for the moment you have all been waiting for. Will the real Calamity Jane step forward.

Answer: #3

Good Reading: *Calamity Jane, Her Life and Legend* by Doris Faber. Houghton Mifflin, 1992; *Calamity Jane: Frontier Original* by William Sanford. Enslow, 1996.

TRANSFORMING NARRATIVE INTO DIALOGUE!

It is possible to create readers theatre scripts from any form of narrative . . . a newspaper article, an Aesop's Fable, a paragraph from the science or social studies text are good examples. There is no expense involved, no props or costumes are used, and the readers theatre group both prepares and performs its own script.

Preparing the Script

Students in the upper primary grades through high school can quickly be taught to turn any piece of narrative writing into a readers theatre script. The procedure is as follows:

1. Read the piece together with each person reading a line in turn.
2. Decide on the characters who will speak.
3. Decide on which characters will need narrators.
4. Narrator speaking parts can be marked N1 for narrator one and N2 for narrator two. Each narrator reads those lines that apply to his or her character.
5. Words that indicate what a character is thinking, feeling, or doing can be spoken by that character. Characters' parts can be indicated with the first letter or letters of the characters' names.
6. NO WORDS IN THE SELECTION ARE CHANGED. The integrity of the text must be kept. However, words or sound effects can be added for emphasis. Study the nonfiction narrative on the next page, and see how it is turned into a readers theatre script.

Frontier Towns

Reading Parts: N1 = Narrator One; N2 = Narrator Two; V = Visitor; M = Miner

N1
Frontier towns sprang up almost overnight. An early arrival in
V
Bovard, Nevada told how he/ passed through the town in the
N1
morning and noticed four or five tents./ When he returned in the
V
afternoon/ Main Street was a mile long and business was
N2
booming in a string of tent saloons./ There were few comforts.
M
A miner/ often slept outdoors in summer, and built a dugout or
N2   **M**
crude shack in the winter./ He might have a tent/ or make a shelter
N2
out of rocks or empty packing cases./ One miner/
M   **N2**
collected all the rocks/ he could find for shelter against the winter.
M
The next spring he discovered/ the walls were high grade silver worth $75,000.

Frontier Towns

(Note: While no words are changed, additional words can be added.)

Reading Parts: Narrator One, Narrator Two, Visitor, Miner

Narrator One: Frontier towns sprang up almost overnight (BOING! BOING! BOING!). An early arrival in Bovard, Nevada told how he

Visitor: passed through the town in the morning and noticed four or five tents.

Narrator One: When he returned in the afternoon *what a sight met his eyes!*

Visitor: Main Street was a mile long and business was booming in a string of tent saloons. *(You'd think miners could find a better way to spend their money.)*

Narrator Two: There were few comforts. A miner

Miner: often slept outdoors in summer, and built a dugout or crude shack in the winter. *(I froze my toes and my nose!)*

Narrator Two: He might have a tent *(if he's lucky)*

Miner: or make a shelter out of rocks or empty packing cases.

Narrator Two: One miner

Miner: collected all the rocks *(oh, my aching back!)*

Narrator Two: for shelter against the winter. The next spring he discovered

Miner: the walls were high grade silver worth $75,000. *Can you believe that?*
I slept surrounded by $75,000 all winter!

All: *So the moral to this story is, Look Before You Sleep!*

NONFICTION BOOKTALKS TO MARK AND PERFORM

Haym Salomon: American Patriot **by Susan Goldman Rubin. Abrams, 2007.**

Everyone knows the Revolutionary War figures George Washington, Benjamin Franklin and Paul Revere, but Haym Salomon was also an important hero and his accomplishments are finally getting recognition. Haym and his wife were among the few Jewish patriots of the time. Along with others, his wife was amazed at his knowledge of languages and currency. She knew he was an exceptional man in pre-Revolution New York. Incredibly valuable to the revolutionary cause, Haym risked his life and his fortune, went to prison, and was forced to abandon his home and family, all for the sake of American independence.

Susanna of the Alamo **by John Jakes. Harcourt, 1986.**

Before dawn on Sunday March 6, Santa Anna's armies were stirring. Dozing in an old damp blanket with Angelina in her arms, Susanna woke suddenly. "What is that music?" she whispered. Guns were crackling outside the chapel. Artillery matches glowed near the cannon on the walls. Susanna stared into the horrified face of her friend, Senora Espanza. "Santa Anna is tormenting us," the Senora replied. "The music means, "Show No Mercy! Kill Everyone?" Sharp as knives the bugle notes flew through the air. Susanna clutched her baby. She heard shouting and ladders thumping against the Alamo walls. Susanna's heart beat fast. She looked at the women. All the faces shared the same look. They seemed to say, "We are frightened but we stayed here to show what we were made of. Now it is time."

Black and White Airmen: Their True History **by John Fleischman. Houghton-Mifflin, 2007.**

Here is the true history of a friendship that almost wasn't. John Leahr and Herb Heilbrun grew up in the same neighborhood and were in the same third grade class together. They were classmates, not friends, because Herb was white and John was black.

John and Herb were twenty-one when the United States entered World War II. Herb became an Army Air Forces B-17 pilot. John flew P-51 fighters. Both were thrown into the brutal high-altitude bomber war against Nazi Germany, though they never met because the army was rigidly segregated. Only in the air were black and white American flyers allowed to mix.

Both came safely home but it took Herb and John another fifty years to meet again and discover that their lives had run almost side-by-side through the war and peace. Old friends at last, Herb and John launched a mission to tell young people why race once made all the difference and why it shouldn't any more.

Hurricane Force **by Joseph B. Treaster. Kingfisher Books, 2007.**

Joe Treaster peered through the lattice of the New Orleans police headquarters parking garage. He was watching the devastating power of a hurricane up close. Packing winds of 118 miles per hour, Hurricane Katrina is attacking New Orleans, uprooting trees, tearing down power lines, and flattening homes. Inside headquarters a policeman answers phones as more and more people, trapped by the rising flood waters ask for help. But rescue workers cannot leave the safety of the building until the hurricane has passed. Water was rising in the downtown streets. Soon it would cover parked cars. The wind and the rain owned the city. The storm had taken over. From this harrowing vantage point Joe Treaster is poised to report on what may prove to be the most infamous storms in American history.

GOOD READING: AMERICAN HISTORY

Adler, David. *Enemies of Slavery*. Holiday House, 2004.
    Fourteen men and women who fought against slavery in various ways.

Adler, David. *Heroes of the Revolution*. Holiday House, 2004.
    Short tales of heroes from spying on the British to rescuing fallen soldiers.

Ammon, Richard. *Valley Forge*. Holiday House, 2004.
    A stirring account of the winter at Valley Forge in 1778.

Anderson, Marcella and Vollstadt, Elizabeth. *Young Patriots*. Boyds Mill, 2004.
    Fifteen accounts of young people through whose eyes the Revolution unfolds.

Barner, Bob. *Which Way to the Revolution?* Holiday House, 1998.
    When Paul Revere isn't sure which way to go, a band of mice help out. A different information-filled look at the famous ride.

Bial, Raymond. *Ghost Towns of the American West*. Houghton-Mifflin, 2001.
    A history of abandoned towns and why people left.

Davis, Kenneth. *Don't Know Much About the Presidents?* HarperCollins, 2002.
    Presidents' achievements, nicknames, hobbies, favorite foods, and how White House life changed over the years.

Edwards, Judith. *The Great Expedition of Lewis and Clark*. Farrar, 2003.
    The retelling of the expedition as told by Reubin Field.

Ferrie, Richard. *The World Turned Upside Down*. Holiday House, 1999.
    The true story of how a ragtag army, low on food and equipment, managed to defeat the British at the Battle of Yorktown.

Fradin, Dennia. *Let It Begin Here!* Lexington and Concord. Walker, 2005.
    The story of the first battle of the American Revolution.

Filipucci, Laura Francesca. *Blizzard of 1888*. Walker, 2004.
    Free verse brings the blizzard alive showing the hardships when the largest city in the country was shut down.

Friedman, Robin. *The Silent Witness*. Houghton-Mifflin, 2005.
    A true account of a family who saw the Civil War unfold in their home.

Fritz, Jean. *The Lost Colony of Roanoke*. Putnam, 2004.
    What happened to the 115 colonists of Roanoke who disappeared almost without a trace?

Gauch, Patricia Lee. *Thunder at Gettysburg*. Boyds Mill, 2003.
    The Battle of Gettysburg as seen through the eyes of a child.

Harness, Cheryl. *Rabble Rousers*. Dutton, 2003.
  Short biographies of twenty women who made a difference in American life.

Holzer, Harold. *The President is Shot!* Boyds Mill, 2004.
  Answers to questions about the assassination of Abraham Lincoln.

Katz, Susan. *A Revolutionary Field Trip*. Simon & Schuster, 2004.
  Poems of Colonial America.

Keenan, Sheila. *O, Say Can You See: American Symbols and Landmarks*. Scholastic, 2004.
  The stories behind the symbols of America from Plymouth Rock to Mt. Rushmore.

Krensky, Stephen. *Dangerous Crossing*. Dutton, 2005.
  The revolutionary voyage in 1778 of John Quincy Adams on a secret mission to France.

Krull, Kathleen. *A Woman for President: The Story of Victoria Woodhull*. Walker & Co., 2004.
  Supporting her family at the age of eight and later becoming a millionaire, in 1872 she was the first woman to run for president.

Lalicki, Tom. *Grierson's Raid*. Farrar, Strauss & Giroux, 2004.
  A day by day account of the sixteen day raid through Mississippi led by Colonel Benjamin H. Grierson.

Leacock, Elspeth and Buckley, Susan. *Journeys in Time: A New Atlas of American History*. Houghton-Mifflin, 2001.
  Follow the footsteps of real people who made American History.

McKissack, Patricia and Fredrick. *Days of Jubilee*. Scholastic, 2003.
  An account of the days and weeks that followed the end of slavery.

McWorter, Diane. *A Dream of Freedom*. Scholastic, 2004.
  An account of the Civil Rights Movement from 1954 to 1968.

Meltzer, Milton. *Hear that Train Whistle Blow*. Random House, 2004.
  A history of the railroad with emphasis on how it changed society.

Murphy, Claire. *I Am Sacajawea, I Am York*. Walker, 2005.
  Both Sacajawea and the slave, York, proved to be valuable members of the Lewis & Clark expedition.

Rappaport, Doreen. *Victory or Death*. HarperCollins, 2003.
  Exciting stories of the American Revolution.

Sandler, Martin. *America's Great Disasters*. HarperCollins, 2003.
  Accounts of major disasters and the courageous and strong Americans who faced them.

St. George, Judith. *The One and Only Declaration of Independence*. Philomel, 2005.
  The true account of the writing of this famous document.

Stevenson, Harvey. *Looking at Liberty*. HarperCollins, 2003.
  The story of the Statue of Liberty told through verse and paintings.

Tanaka, Shelley. *A Day that Changed America: Earthquake*. Hyperion, 2004.
The story of the San Francisco earthquake of 1906 with dramatic paintings.

Tanaka, Shelley. *D Day*. Hyperion, 2004.
A compelling account of this world-changing day told with real-life stories.

Author / Title Index

Aaron and the Green Mountain Boys, 110
Adler, David, 155
Adventures of Penrose, The, 55
Albert Einstein, 52
All About Alligators, 29
Alligators and Crocodiles, 9
Amato, Mary, 67
Amazing, Impossible Erie Canal, The, 120, 133
Amazing Math Journey, An, 54
America's Great Disasters, 131, 156
Ammon, Richard, 155
Andersen, Hans Christian, 62
Anderson, Marcella, 125, 155
Animal Fact, Animal Fable, 30
Animal Homes, 21
Animal Perception and Communication, 29
Animal Wonders, 31
Annie Oakley, 145
Anno's Mysterious Multiplying Jar, 54
Archimedes: Father of Mathematics, 58
Ardley, Neil, 81
Arithme-Tickle, 67
Arnosky, Jim, 10
Around the World in a Hundred Years, 91
Art of Keeping Cool, The, 121
Ask Dr. K. Fisher About Animals, 21
Atkins, Jeanine, 18

Barefoot, 125
Barner, Bob, 136, 155
Barnstormers and Daredevils, 138
Beatty, Richard, 19
Bender, Lionel, 131
Berger, Gilda, 18
Berger, Melvin, 18
Berkes, Marianne, 106
Best Book of Fossils, Rocks and Minerals, The, 30
Beyond the Divide, 121
Bial, Raymond, 155
Bill Gates, 61
Billy Yank and Johnny Reb, 127
Bishop, Nic, 21
Black and White Airmen, 153

Blizzard of 1888, 126, 155
Blunder or Brainstorm, 25, 26
Bones, Bones, Dinosaur Bones, 28
Bosak, Susan, 8
Boston Tea Party, The, 136
Bowen, Gary, 122
Boy and His Bear, A, 121
Boys' War, The, 127
Branley, Franklyn, 36
Brenner, Barbara, 112
Brimner, Larry Dane, 141
Brown, Don, 106
Buck Stops Here, The, 120
Buckley, Susan, 156
Buffalo Bill and the Pony Express, 136, 143
By the Dawn's Early Light, 110

Calamity Jane, Frontier Original, 147
Calamity Jane, Her Life, and Legend, 147
Can You Guess?, 67
Canada from A to Z, 93
Caribbean Counting Book, 92
Case of the Monkeys That Fell from the Trees, The, 21
Cassie's Sweet Berry Pie, 111
Celebrating the Fifty States, 79, 88
Challen, Paul, 87
Chemically Active, 29
Cheney, Lynne, 122
Chrismer, Melanie, 67
Chuck Yeager Breaks the Sound Barrier, 132
Circle of Fire, 121
City of Snow, 90
City Not Forsaken, 90
Clara Barton & Her Victory Over Fear, 147
Clements, Andrew, 67
Clemson, Wendy, 67
Cobb, Vicki, 14
Coerr, Eleanor, 136, 143
Collard, Sneed, III, 106
Collection of Mathematical Adventures, A, 53
Come All You Brave Soldiers, 127
Come Back Salmon, 29

Computers Then and Now, 59
Conlon-McKenna, Marita, 113
Counting Caterpillars, 95
Covered Wagons, Bumpy Trails, 115
Craig, Peter, 61
Creatures of Earth, Sea and Sky, 21
Crinkleroot's Guide to Knowing Animal Habitats, 10
Cross, Diana, 34
Croswell, Ken, 18
Curlee, Lynn, 86, 106

D Day, 156
Dangerous Crossing, 123, 156
Daniel Boone, 124
Daugherty, James, 124
Davis, Kenneth, 18, 155
Davy Crockett, 141
Davy Crockett at the Alamo, 120
Day It Rained Forever, The, 138
Day That Changed America, A, 156
Days of Jubilee, 156
Death of the Iron Horse, 120
Dewey, Jennifer, 21
Dinosaur World, 24
Dinosaur Discoveries, 23
Dinosaurs, 24
Dinosaurs Down Under, 29
Dinosaurs of Waterhouse Watkins, 24
Dinosaurs! Strange and Wonderful, 24
Dinosaurs to Dodos, 24
Dixon, Dougal, 24
Do Stars Have Points?, 18
Dog Came, Too, A, 124
Don't Know Much About Space?, 18
Don't Know Much About the Presidents?, 155
Door in the Wall, The, 121
Dot and the Line, The, 55
Dougal Dixon's Amazing Dinosaurs, 24
Dougal Dixon's Dinosaurs, 24
Dr. Jekyll & Mr. Hyde, 32
Dream of Freedom, A, 156
Dudley, Karen, 9
Dyson, Marianne, 18

Earle, Sylvia, 31
Earth keepers, 28
Earthday, 31
Earthquake (picture book), 137
Earthquakes, 137

Earthshake, 106
Earthsong, 106
Edwards, Judith, 155
Edwards, Pamela Duncan, 125, 136
Egger-Bovet, Howard, 123
Endangered Animals, 31
Enemies of Slavery, 155
Encyclopedia of Animals, 19
Environmental Disaster, 87
Escape from Slavery, 111
Even Steven and Odd Todd, 54
Everyone Uses Math, 67
Explorer, 71
Explorer's Handbook, The, 134
Exploring Your Solar System, 18

Faber, Doris, 149
Far Beyond the Garden Gate, 106
Faustin, Charles, 92
Ferrie, Richard, 155
Filipucci, Laura Francesca, 126, 155
Fleischman, John, 153
Flash, Crash, Rumble and Roll, 28
Forbes, Esther, 110
Fractals, Googols and Other Mathematical Tales, 55
Fradin, Dennis, 116, 155
Fredericks, Anthony, 7
Friedman, Dennis, 155
Fritz, Jean, 91, 155
From Sea to Shining Sea, 120
Frozen Man, 28

G is for Googol, 54
Galaxies, 18
Galvin, Jack, 106
Garland, Sherry, 137
Garrett, Ginger, 5
Gauch, Patricia Lee, 155
George versus George, 127
Ghost Towns of the American West, 155
Gibbons, Gail, 23, 72
Give Me Liberty!, 127
Global Warming, 106
Gow, Mary, 58
Grapes of Math, The, 54, 67
Great Expedition of Lewis and Clark, The, 155
Great Fire, The, 131
Great Northern Diver: The Loon, 29
Great Turkey Walk, The, 121

Greedy Triangle, The, 54
Grierson's Raid, 156
Gross, Virginia T., 138

Hansen, Joyce, 110
Harcourt, Lalie, 57
Harness, Cheryl, 133, 156
Harrison, David, 85
Hatkoff, Isabella, 21
Haym Salomon, American Patriot, 109, 153
Hear that Train Whistle Blow, 133, 156
Heard, Georgia, 21
Hemans, Felicia, 118
Heroes of the Revolution, 155
Henry, Michael, 22, 23, 24
Hidden Worlds: Looking Through a Scientist's Microscope, 4
High, Linda, 90
Hillard, Richard, 18. 30
Hold the Flag High, 127
Holzer, Harold, 156
Homespun Sarah, 115
Hottest, Coldest, Highest, Deepest, 80, 106
Hour of Freedom: American History in Poetry, 118
House of Wisdom, The, 121
How Heavy Is It?, 67
How Much Is a Million?, 55, 67
How to Think Like a Scientist, 6
Hurricane Force, 154
Hynes, Margaret, 30

I Am Sacajawea, I Am York, 156
If You Hopped Like a Frog, 21
If You Were There in 1776, 127
If Your Name Was Changed at Ellis Island, 138
In Code, 54
Into the Ice Age, 86, 106
Invention, 31
Iron Horses, 115, 137

Jakes, John, 129, 153
Jaguar in the Rain Forest, 21
Janice Van Cleve's Geometry for Every Kid, 48
Jenkins, Steve, 80, 82, 106
Jericho's Journey, 112
Johnny Tremain, 110
Jonas Salk, 38
Journey to the Planets, 28
Journeys in Time, 156

Kalman, Bobbie, 93
Kara's New World, 120
Kate Crackernuts, 64-66
Katz, Susan, 156
Kay, Verla, 115, 137, 139
Keenan, Sheila, 156
Kellogg, Steven, 112
Kerley, Barbara, 24
Knights of the Kitchen Table, 56
Kramer, Stephen, 46
Krensky, Steven, 123, 145, 156
Kroll, Steven, 110
Krull, Kathleen, 156
Kumin, Maxine, 24

Lakin, Patricia, 52
Lalicki, Tom, 156
Lamp, the Ice and the Boat Called Fish*, The*, 106
Landau, Elaine, 31
Landing of the Pilgrim Fathers, The, 118
Lauber, Patricia, 11
Last Princess, The, 120
Leacock, Elspeth, 156
Lee, Milly, 137
Leedy, Loreen, 17, 79, 88
Lessem, Don, 24
Levine, Ellen, 138
Let It Begin Here: Lexington and Concord, 116, 155
Lewis, J. Patrick, 106
Llewellyn, Claire, 21
Life and Times of the Honeybee, 28
Lily and Miss Liberty, 120
Long Road to Gettysburg, The, 127
Looking at Liberty, 156
Lost Colony of Roanoke, 155
Lourie, Peter, 84

Man Who Counted, The, 55
Manson, Ainslie, 124
Martin, Jacqueline Briggs, 106
Math Appeal, 67
Math at the Store, 67
Math Curse, 46, 57
Math Fables, 67
Math Games Around the World, 54
Math in the Backyard, 67
Math in the Car, 67
Math in the Kitchen, 67
Math in the Neighborhood, 67
Math on the Playground, 67

Math Potatoes, 67
Math-Terpieces, 67
Math Trek, 55
Matthews, Rupert, 71
McDonald, Megan, 123
McGrath, Barbara, 81
McKissack, Patricia, 156
McKissack, Fredrick, 156
McLeese, Don, 38, 60
McWorter, Diane, 156
Meltzer, Milton, 118, 133, 156
Messages from Mars, 17
Mike Fink, 112
Million Dots, A, 67
Mind Stretching Math Riddles, 54
Mississippi River, 84
Mites to Mastodons, 24
Moon in Bear's Eyes, 21
Morpurgo, Michael, 113
Morris, Gilbert, 90
Morris, Lynn, 90
Money Box, 62
Mountains, 30
Mr. Lincoln's Drummer Boy, 111
Multiply This!, 67
Mummy Math, 67
Murphy, Claire, 156
Murphy, Jim, 83, 131
My Face in the Wind: A Prairie Teacher, 83
Myers, Jack, 24
Mysteries of the Universe, 36

National Geographic Atlas of the World, 79
Neil, Buzz and Mike Go to the Moon, 18, 30
Nettie's Trip South, 120
Neuschwander, Cindy, 53, 56, 57
Number Devil, The, 54
No Hero for the Kaiser, 120

O, Say Can You See?: American Symbols and Landmarks, 156
O'Dell, Scott, 106, 113
On Beyond a Million, 54, 67
One and Only Declaration of Independence, The, 116, 156
One Hundred Angry Ants, 55
1000 Years Ago on Planet Earth, 106
Operation Grizzly Bear, 28
Oppenheim, Shulamith, 18
Orphan Train, 115
Over in the Ocean, 106

Owen and Mzee: The Language of Friendship, 21

Path of the Pale Horse, 121
Pecos Bill, 112
Pellant, Chris, 30
Peters, Lisa, 106
Pews, Bill, 112
Pfetzer, Mark, 106
Photographic Story of Hatching, A, 29
Pigs Will Be Pigs, 54
Planet Earth Inside Out, 72
Planets, 31
Planets in Our Solar System, 18
Polette, Nancy, 25
President is Shot!, The, 156
Pringle, Laurence, 24, 106

Rabble Rousers, 156
Rand McNally Atlas of the World, 75, 76, 77, 78
Rappaport, Doreen, 111, 156
Raptor: The Life of a Young Deinonychus, 22, 23
Rathbun, Elizabeth, 18
Red Riding Hood's Math Adventure, 57
Revolutionary Field Trip, A, 156
Rio Grande, 84
Rivers: Nature's Wondrous Waterways, 85
Robert Goddard, 60
Rogers, Sally, 106
Rubin, Susan Goldman, 109, 153
Ruffin, Frances, 145
Rumford, James, 106
Rybeck, Carol, 31
Ryder, Joanne, 21

Safari Park, 54
Sandler, Martin, 131, 156
Sanford, William, 149
Sargent, Brian, 67
Saving the Liberty Bell, 123
Schuerger, Andrew, 17
Schwartz, David M., 21, 67
Science Book of Motion, The, 29
Science Book of Weather, 81
Science Discoveries on the Net, 7
Science Experiments You Can Eat, 28
Science Is . . . , 8
Scientists Ask Questions, 5
Scieszka, Jon, 46, 56, 57
Sea Critters, 31
Secrets of Animal Flight, The, 21

See and Spy Counting, 55
See For Yourself, 14
See the Stars, 18
Serpent Never Sleeps, The, 109
Silent Witness, The, 127, 155
Shooting for the Moon, 145
Simon, Seymour, 18, 30, 97, 137
Sing Down the Moon, 113
Sir Cumference and the Dragon, 67
Sir Cumference and the First Round Table, 56, 67
Sir Cumference and the Great Knight of Angleland, 67
Sir Cumference and the Sword in the Cone, 67
Smith-Barabzini, Marlene, 123
Some Plants Have Funny Names, 34
Space Station Science, 18
St. George, Judith, 116, 156
Star of Fear, Star of Hope, 121
Stein, Conrad, 132
Stories Science Photos Tell, 29
Storm, The, 81
Stranded at Plimouth Plantation, 1626, 122
Strange Mysteries from Around the World, 97
Stevenson, Harvey, 156
Stevenson, Robert Louis, 32
Susanna of the Alamo, 129, 153
Swinburne, Stephen, 21, 30

Tanaka, Shelley, 156
Tang, Greg, 67
Tattered Sails, 115, 139
Tessendorf, K.C., 138
Then What Happened, Paul Revere?, 120
Thunder at Gettysburg, 155
Tiger Math, 55
Tolhurst, Marilyn, 134
Top of the World: Climbing Mt. Everest, 28, 82
Traveling Man, 106
Treaster, Joseph B., 154
Turtle Tide, 30
Twist of Gold, 113
Two Eyes, a Nose and a Mouth, 29

U. S. Kids History, 123
Ultimate Interactive Atlas of the World, The, 75, 76, 77, 78

Under the Ground, 28
United No More!, 127
Using Math to Be a Zoo Vet, 67
Using Math to Conquer Extreme Sports, 67
Using Math to Solve a Crime, 67

Valley Forge, 155
Van Cleve, Janis, 48
Vast Mysterious Deep, The, 85
Victory or Death, 156
Voices of the Alamo, 137
Vollstadt, Elizabeth, 125, 155

Wagon Wheels, 112
Weber, Rebecca, 59
Wexo, John, 31
What Does the Crow Know?, 29
What Happened to the Mammoths?, 24
What Is the Full Moon Full Of?, 18
What the Dinosaurs Saw, 24
When Washington Crossed the Delaware, 122
Where Did the Butterfly Get It's Name?, 9
Which Way Freedom, 110
Which Way to the Revolution?, 136, 155
White Bear, Ice Bear, 21
Who Eats What?, 11
Why Can't You Unscramble an Egg?, 28
Wildflower Girl, 113
Wildlife Rescue, 21
Wilkes, Angela, 21
Wings and Rockets, 18
Wings Around the World, 121
Winnick, Karen, 111
Winter Whale, 21
Wish Me Luck, 121
Wisler, G. Clifton, 111, 112
Within Reach: My Everest Story, 106
Woman for President, A, 156
World Almanac for Kids, 94
World of Wonders, 106
World Turned Upside Down, 127, 155
Wortzman, Ricki, 57

Yankee Doodle America, the Spirit of 1776, 127
Young Patriots, 125, 155
Young People's Book of Space, 18

About the Author

NANCY POLETTE is an educator with over 30 years experience. She has authored over 150 professional books. She lives and works in Missouri, where she is Professor at Lindenwood College.